faith, family, friends, dating, and more

girls of grace

Q&A

with Point of Grace
and Nancy Alcorn of Mercy Ministries

HOWARD
PUBLISHING CO.

Our purpose at Howard Publishing is to:
- *Increase faith* in the hearts of growing Christians
- *Inspire holiness* in the lives of believers
- *Instill hope* in the hearts of struggling people everywhere
Because He's coming again!

Q & A © 2005 by Point of Grace
All rights reserved. Printed in the United States of America
Published by Howard Publishing Co., Inc.
3117 North Seventh Street, West Monroe, Louisiana 71291-2227
www.howardpublishing.com

05 06 07 08 09 10 11 12 13 14   10 9 8 7 6 5 4 3 2 1

Edited by Beth Lueders
Interior design by Stephanie D. Walker
Cover design by LinDee Loveland
Cover photo by Aaron Rapoport

Library of Congress Cataloging-in-Publication Data

Q & A with Point of Grace: faith, family, friends, dating, and more / girls of Grace and
Nancy Alcorn.
    p. cm.
  ISBN 1-58229-463-1
    1. Christian girls—Religious life—Miscellanea. 2. Teenage girls—Religious life—Miscellanea.
I. Title: Question and answer with Point of Grace. II. Alcorn, Nancy. III. Point of Grace.
(Musical Group)

BV4551.3.Q22 2005
248.8'33—dc22

                                                                            2005050237

The information contained in this book does not constitute professional or clinical advice. We've tried to provide quality help, but make no claims, promises, or guarantees as to the accuracy, completeness, or adequacy of the information. As clinical advice must be tailored to the specific individuals and circumstances of each case, and society and other influences are constantly changing, this should not be used as a substitute for advice of one's own licensed professional.

We'd like to dedicate this book to our wonderful mothers—
Brenda, Janice, Robin, and Sharon—
who always allow us to ask the hard questions
and answer honestly in wisdom, love, and kindness.

Contents

Contents

Introduction

May God, the source of hope, fill you with joy
and peace through your faith in him.
Romans 15:13

Thank you for inviting us into your life through the pages of this book.
Every year we meet thousands of teenage girls around the country—many
of them just like you—who long to follow God while struggling with
everyday pressures and troubling circumstances.

Some of these girls tell us secrets they have been too afraid to verbalize
to anyone else. Others just need a little reassurance "that all things work
together for the good of those who love God" (Romans 8:28). No matter
how old we are, we all have questions, fears, and longings. At times we all
wonder if God truly understands what we experience on this earth. We are
here to tell you that He does!

Psalm 139:1–5 describes God's intimate knowledge of you. "O LORD,
you have examined me, and you know me. You alone know when I sit
down and when I get up. You read my thoughts from far away. You watch
me when I travel and when I rest. You are familiar with all my ways. Even
before there is a [single] word on my tongue, you know all about it, LORD.
You are all around me—in front of me and in back of me. You lay your
hand on me."

God knows your thoughts and feelings even before you express them.
He knows how you feel about boys. He understands when you're unhappy
with your body. He sees your disagreements with your parents. He realizes
your desire to live out your faith. He also knows that you need counsel,
comfort, and hope for the problems and decisions you face.

1

This book is a collection of transparent, real-life questions from teenage girls we've encountered through our concerts and Girls of Grace conferences. Although we don't know the full circumstances behind every girl's question, we have each studied God's Word and prayed for His guidance to answer these questions with wisdom, sensitivity, and truth. You'll also gain insight through the experiences of our close friend Nancy Alcorn, whose ministry walks alongside thousands of confused and hurting young girls.

Because some of your uncertainties and problems may stem from deeper issues within, you may need a thorough medical checkup or professional support to help you. Please reach out for all the help you need—you are worth it! You are precious to God and to us. Rest assured that we, too, have faced many of your same awkward, anxious, and annoying struggles.

You are continually on our hearts and minds, and we pray for God to use this book to encourage and uphold you. May "God's peace, which goes beyond anything we can imagine . . . guard your thoughts and emotions through Christ Jesus" (Philippians 4:7).

With grateful hearts,
Denise, Heather, Leigh, Shelley

Dating

Q&A

My boyfriend is *way* too clingy and is *always* all over me— even at church. How do I tell him to stop without him breaking up with me?

Well, unfortunately there is no way to promise he won't break up with you. But, if he desires to follow the Lord, then your boyfriend will be willing to hear you out. You must talk to your guy about how uncomfortable you feel. Sit him down and speak from your heart. You can speak truth without being mean.

Crowding someone in a relationship is often a sign of deeper fears and insecurities. Perhaps you can help your boyfriend explore why he's overly dependent on you. If you don't address your concerns now, your relationship will only suffer. If your boyfriend is clingy in public, then how he acts alone with you can lead to a much bigger problem.

I know it's hard to think about breaking up with someone, but all our relationships are to glorify God. If you are already feeling a check in your spirit that things aren't quite right, then it could be the Holy Spirit guiding you away from this relationship.

—*Denise*

He who speaks truth tells what is right.
PROVERBS 12:17 NASB

Q&A

Is it OK to date a non-Christian boy in hope of bringing him to the Lord?

Have you heard the saying, "It is easier for someone to push you down than for someone to pull you up"? This describes what happens when you are at opposite levels spiritually with a boy. In 2 Corinthians 6:14, God advises Christians to "not be yoked together with unbelievers" (NIV). Does this mean we are to isolate ourselves from nonbelievers? No, not at all; if we did, we could not carry out God's plan for us to tell others about Jesus (see Matthew 28:18–20). God's instruction in 2 Corinthians 6 means believers should avoid situations that would force them to divide their loyalties or compromise their faith.

The question is: can you be assured that this guy will become a Christian while you are dating him? The answer to that is no. You cannot predict another person's response to the good news—that is God's job. I suggest you share the love of Christ with this boy and invite him to your youth group or church, but do not lock yourself into a personal relationship that could cause you to compromise your beliefs or convictions. "Above all else, guard your heart, for it is the wellspring of life" (Proverbs 4:23 NIV).

—*Leigh*

Do not be yoked together with unbelievers.
For what do righteousness and wickedness have in common?
Or what fellowship can light have with darkness?
2 CORINTHIANS 6:14 NIV

7

Q&A

How do you know if a boy likes you or not?

I don't know if there is a definite way to tell if a boy likes you or not. When you were younger, boys would be rude and hit you if they liked you, but they grow out of this behavior in their teenage years. If a boy is paying extra attention to you or telling you how nice you look, or if you catch him looking at you at odd times, these could be signs that he likes you. He might also stumble over his words or act silly when he's with you. His face might even turn red. Just make sure that he loves Jesus before you go out with him.

—*Heather*

Discretion will protect you, and understanding will guard you.
PROVERBS 2:11 NIV

Q&A

How do you talk to a guy you like when you're too nervous to even look at him and he really doesn't even notice you?

First of all, honor your own personality. If you are by nature a shy person, then I wouldn't recommend forcing yourself to initiate a conversation. Even if you're like me and have the mouth, just not the guts, breaking the ice can still feel awkward. Why not start by praying and asking God for an opportunity to make speaking to this guy seem natural. Then muster up your courage the best you can—and just go for it! What have you got to lose?

Perhaps you could simply say, "John, I know I don't even know you, but I just wanted to tell you I think you're a cool guy. I know that might sound weird or whatever, but I just wanted to say hey." That's exactly what I would do if I were dying to talk to a guy who didn't notice me. I guarantee you, if "John" is someone you want to know, he will probably think you're a cool girl for being so vulnerable without being pushy. He can take things from there.

—Shelley

Be strong, all who wait with hope for the LORD,
and let your heart be courageous.
PSALM 31:24

9

Q&A

I'm thirteen. Is it OK for me to date a sixteen-year-old guy, even if my parents don't know?

Without going any further, I see a red flag. Don't do anything behind your parents' backs. This is deceitful and not honoring to God or to your parents. I'm not your mom or dad, and I don't know the full situation, but if you were my daughter, you wouldn't be dating *anyone* at the age of thirteen. Maybe I'm old-fashioned, but I don't think thirteen-year-olds should be dating. When you're thirteen, it's hard enough to adjust to all the changes that come with entering the teenage years without adding the pressures that dating brings.

Thirteen is too young to make the kinds of decisions that you have to make in a dating relationship. Let me clarify—I'm not saying that you can't have a boyfriend. That decision should be made between your parents and you. But dating and meeting your boyfriend at the mall on Saturday with a group of friends are two different things. And even if you do meet a boy at the mall with friends, make sure you're honest with your parents about it, and don't be one-on-one with him. Stay in groups.

—*Heather*

Integrity and honesty will protect me because I wait for you.
PSALM 25:21

Q&A

What do you think of a sixteen-year-old girl dating a twenty-five-year-old guy?

Let's think about this one together. It's not unusual for teenage girls to be attracted to older guys (girls mature faster and often wish guys their own age would "just grow up"). But a nine-year age difference is a *big* deal in dating when one of you is still a teenager.

When you are sixteen, you are still learning about the world and how relationships work. A sixteen-year-old's life typically revolves around attending school, getting a driver's license, and having fun. A twenty-five-year-old guy is an adult, experiencing life on a totally different level.

If you are this sixteen-year-old, you need to get out of the relationship immediately. At this stage in your life you need to enjoy friendships with guys close to your own age. Besides, any twenty-five-year-old who would even consider dating a sixteen-year-old spells trouble!

—*Shelley*

Make your ear attentive to wisdom, incline your heart to understanding.
PROVERBS 2:2 NASB

Q&A

What are some guidelines for safe, healthy, fun, God-glorifying dating relationships?

First and foremost, you both need to have a relationship with Jesus, not just go to church. Go out in groups with friends that have your same values. Limit time alone together. Go bowling, play catch at the park, enjoy each other's company without having to be "physical" with one another. When your date brings you home, go on inside and have a parent be around when the boy comes in. Be sure not to focus so seriously on a thriving dating life.

Keep others in your life, not just "the boyfriend." So many girls I know who have boyfriends seem to forget that their girlfriends exist. Keep Jesus the closest to your heart and have an adult with whom you can be accountable. The guy you date today more than likely will not be your husband, so don't do anything you'd be ashamed to admit to your future husband or uncomfortable doing if Jesus were physically sitting there with you.

—*Denise*

The fear of the LORD is the beginning of wisdom.
Good sense is shown by everyone who follows [God's guiding principles.]
PSALM 111:10

Q&A

Dating is supposed to help a girl find a possible husband, but we all know that most people don't marry their high-school sweethearts. So what's the point of a Christian girl dating in high school?

Well, ironically both my sisters married their high-school sweethearts. However, you're right; it is rare. But I believe dating provides an opportunity to develop relationships with others, while learning about oneself. Looking back on my experiences, all my dating relationships brought something positive into my eventual marriage. For example, one boyfriend demonstrated qualities of true friendship and loyalty toward others. One modeled respect toward his parents that was extremely motivating. Another guy was so funny, which helped me recognize humor as an important characteristic and encouraged me to look for this trait in a spouse. Another simply taught me about cars. These are only a few things that I gained from dating.

Dating is up to you and your parents, but I think it can be an important piece to a successful marriage, as well as help you develop positive social skills.

—*Leigh*

Pursue faith, love, and peace together with those who worship the Lord with a pure heart.
2 TIMOTHY 2:22

Q&A

What do you think about dating in groups instead of couples only?

This is a great idea. That's how I dated all through high school, and honestly, it's a great way to guard you from temptation. You can have a great time going out in groups because there so many things to do that are much more fun with a group of people (bowling, concerts, amusement parks, etc.).

If you do go out on a date alone, it's always a good idea to have at least one older woman (mentor) who is a strong Christian to keep you accountable. Allow that person to ask you the hard questions about what went on during your date. It's also extremely important to set boundaries for yourself before you ever start dating, and then to remind yourself what those boundaries are before you go out on each date. Once you're on a date it's too late to start deciding your boundaries.

Another great way to guard yourself from any compromising situations is to pray with your date before you go out. Ask the Lord to bless your time together. This will hopefully keep your mind focused on glorifying God on your date. If you do go out alone, keep one thing in mind—stay out of dark places!

—*Heather*

*Carefully walk a straight path,
and all your ways will be secure.*
PROVERBS 4:26

Q&A

Is it OK to date someone online?

I'm assuming that if you want to date someone online, you do not live in the same town as this person. I would wave a big red flag to online dating. First of all, "online dating" is a misnomer because it isn't even possible to really *date* someone over the Internet. The Web can be very deceitful, and I believe the Enemy is having his way with young girls through this medium. Even for single adults, online matching services with elaborate screening features cannot fully eliminate troublesome people from exploiting someone.

Think about it. The person you are communicating with via computer can tell you anything he wants, and it's very hard to tell fact from fiction when you are not having face-to-face, heart-to-heart fellowship with that person. I'm not saying you shouldn't communicate with your friends from time to time online, but I would give a definite no to meeting and "dating" people over the Internet. It's not safe, and it's certainly not an authentic relationship in the way God intended.

—*shelley*

My dear brothers and sisters, don't be fooled.
JAMES 1:16

Q&A

What is the difference between dating and courting, and what are your views on the two?

Courting is where the boy asks permission from your parents to spend time with you. More than likely he wants to spend time with you at your house with your family or with others such as a youth group. Dating is going out to places together and is typically a more informal way to get to know the opposite sex. There is a place for both courting and dating, and they can look similar. The most important thing to ask is: am I glorifying God in this relationship?

You can get to know a guy within both scenarios, but you must put more guidelines in place when dating, because you might not always be around other people. Either way, God needs to come first. In high school there really isn't that much of a reason to ever go on dates with just the two of you. Keep your process of getting to know each other simple. This will take the pressure off you both.

— Denise

He has reserved priceless wisdom for decent people.
He is a shield for those who walk in integrity.
PROVERBS 2:7

Friends

Q&A

My friend's boyfriend is cheating on her. How do I tell her without losing her as a friend? Another friend tried to tell her, and now they're not friends anymore.

Being a friend sometimes means being honest even though it may hurt. If you truly care for this girl and you know for sure that her boyfriend is cheating on her, then you must tell her the truth.

First, start by praying ahead of time for the conversation you'll have with your friend. Pray that God will help you share this information in a way that your friend will see that you have no ulterior motives. Pray for God to prepare your friend's heart for your conversation.

It is difficult to receive news that you don't want to hear. Sometimes it takes a little while for a person's heart to receive and process tough information. Don't be shocked if your friend is defensive and angry. But if you continue to love her, eventually she will see that you were only trying to be her friend. If she chooses to think otherwise, that is her issue, not yours. Your part is just to continue to love, even if it's not returned.

—Denise

The one who walks with integrity, does what is righteous, and speaks the truth within his heart . . . will never be shaken.
PSALM 15:2

18

Q&A

How do you help settle a friend's argument with someone in a Christian way without getting in the middle of it?

It's quite commendable that you want to help your friend. I suggest you see your role as an encourager. Let your friend know that because you care, you want what is best for him or her. A broken relationship is not what's best, because it can often hinder our relationship with God.

Encourage your friend to think reasonably and rationally, to find a point of compromise with the person. Let your friend know you're not taking sides; instead, you want to see resolution. Try to see if you can direct both parties to a place of common ground. Remember, living in peace and harmony does not always mean we agree, but it does mean we come to a place of respect and coexistence.

—*Leigh*

Blessed are those who make peace.
They will be called God's children.
MATTHEW 5:9

Q&A

How do you tell people they're wrong without sounding stuck-up?

Honestly, it's all in how you present yourself. When you show other people that you respect them, then most of the time others will respect you in return. You should always listen well and weigh what other people say. Sometimes it's hard to voice a differing view, but you need to stay true to what you know is right.

Consider that there may be some truth in what others say. Even if you still don't agree, you have at least given them a chance to present their case, and now you can tell them why you disagree. I hate it when people just like to disagree instead of having a valid reason to disagree. So, if you are going to tell people they're wrong, let your words be full of grace, and have a sound basis for disagreeing.

—Heather

Let your conversation be always full of grace, seasoned with salt, so that you may know how to answer everyone.
COLOSSIANS 4:6 NIV

Q&A

If your friends still do the things you used to do (that is, the bad things), should you still hang out with them or find new friends?

It's important once you become a Christian and really start living your life for Christ not to alienate your former friends. If you all of a sudden just stop being there for these friends, that doesn't say much for your newfound faith. You will appear judgmental and even hypocritical. But you can be friends with people on an emotional level and not have to hang out with them on Friday nights, if you know what I mean.

For instance, if your old friends are drinking or smoking, not only should you not be doing these things, you shouldn't be in their presence when they're doing these things. Why tempt yourself? And besides that, as a Christian, you have *two* reputations to protect: yours and Christ's.

You should find new friends that share your beliefs so you can be positively influenced and have people to hang out with, while remaining "available" and open to show love to your friends who don't share your convictions.

—*Shelley*

You used to live that kind of sinful life. . . . You've gotten rid of the person you used to be and the life you used to live, and you've become a new person. This new person is continually renewed in knowledge to be like its Creator.
COLOSSIANS 3:7–10

Q&A

My best friend thinks she has to have a boyfriend all the time; and when she doesn't, she thinks her life is over. How can I help her?

First of all, you need to pray for your friend. If she's not a Christian, then it's no wonder she's continually looking for love. She might not want to hear what you have to say, but if you approach her with the right spirit, she will ponder your words. Question your heart, as well, to make sure your motives are pure.

Find some time for the two of you to talk. Take your friend to lunch or have her spend the night. Tell her everything you love about her—things she's good at, your favorite qualities in her, etc. Remind this special friend that all of her great strengths come from the Lord. You might want to ask her what it is that makes her want a boyfriend so much. Let your friend think on this.

Tell your friend how much you love her with or without a boyfriend. She will have to come to her own conclusions after this. You are not responsible for your friend's choices, but you can continue to pray that God will work on her heart while you continue to be a loyal buddy.

—Denise

A friend always loves, and a brother is born to share trouble.
PROVERBS 17:17

Q&A

How do I help a friend who is struggling with sex, drinking, and drugs? She gets mad when I get upset about what she's done and tells me to just let her make her own decisions. Do I need to just back off?

For you to be upset with your friend's behavior is what the Bible calls "righteous anger" and is completely normal. What should you do now is the question. Take your justifiable anger and channel it in another direction. Maybe ask your friend over to your house or go for a walk. During that visit, let her know that you love her and only want to help her. Consider the possibility that your friend is being rebellious for a reason, and she may need a safe place (a friend like you) to confide why she's engaging in risky behavior. Let her talk.

Try to be patient with your friend instead of angry with her. Ephesians 4:2 reminds us, "Be completely humble and gentle; be patient, bearing with one another in love" (NIV). If you continue to be her true friend, she just might come around and begin to make better choices. Now, if your friend is putting her life or someone else's in jeopardy, you may need to confide in both your and your friend's parents. Caution: This will not be easy for her parents to hear, but in the end, they will thank you.

—Leigh

If one falls, the other can help his friend get up. But how tragic it is for the one who is [all] alone when he falls. There is no one to help him get up.
ECCLESIASTES 4:10

Q&A

I have a friend who shows her body way too much. How can I tell her nicely that she needs to dress more modestly?

Sadly, too many Christian young ladies lack modesty. I know it's a struggle because all the stores are filled with revealing, body-hugging clothes. How we dress says a lot about who we are.

First, we have to ask ourselves, "Am I glorifying God?" The ultimate reason to dress modestly and appropriately is to glorify God. God advises us in 1 Corinthians 6:20 to "glorify God in your body" (NASB). Second, remember that God wired guys differently than girls. Girls are stimulated by touch and emotion. Boys are stimulated by what they see.

If you and your friend want to date and marry Christian young men, then you need to consider that how you dress will affect who you attract. If you want a boy to respect you, then you must dress in a respectful way. If you want a guy to know where you stand on sexual purity, then how you dress had better line up with what you say. Also, don't ever try to sneak out of the house wearing something that you know your parents won't approve of; instead, trust your parents' opinion and honor what they say.

—*Heather*

Don't you know that your body is a temple that belongs to the Holy Spirit?
The Holy Spirit, whom you received from God, lives in you.
You don't belong to yourselves. You were bought for a price.
So bring glory to God in the way you use your body.
1 Corinthians 6:19–20

Q&A

I believe I have God in my heart, and I have friends who say they have Him in theirs. But they do stupid things, and sometimes I go along with them. What should I do?

Here's the deal: You will never be a perfect Christian. God just wants you to do the very best you can in life. The truth is, sometimes we all do "stupid" things that go against our good judgment. When you make a mistake, recognize it, repent of it (admit your sin to God and tell Him you're sorry), and turn the other way. You can feel good about the fact that you know when you "mess up."

The next time you're considering going along with your friends—when you know you shouldn't—remember the words of Proverbs 14:12, "There is a way that seems right to a person, but eventually it ends in death." Choosing the right path is a great thing to model to your friends, and together you can help each other make wise choices.

—Shelley

God is faithful and reliable. If we confess our sins, he forgives them and cleanses us from everything we've done wrong.
1 JOHN 1:9

Q&A

How can I talk to my friends about Jesus without sounding weird, uptight, and churchy? What words do I use?

Talking about Jesus with others can be scary. I've found that the more connected I am with God, the easier it is for my faith to come out naturally in my conversations. Spiritual talk may sound weird to some of your friends, so communicating how God is working in your life will make Jesus more real to them. You can simply say, "I was so stressed out about my test today. I prayed about it, and God helped me relax and trust that things would be OK."

Pray for and be aware of opportunities to talk about God. Then just share what drew you to Jesus. It's your story that will interest your friends. If your friends ask something about God you don't know—it's OK! Tell them you'll find out and get back to them. Or see if your friends are willing to meet with your youth pastor or other Christian leader.

It's also a good idea to write out the details of your journey of faith, so you have a clear picture of how to communicate your story when the time comes. It's God's job to save your friends. You are simply to tell your story.

—*Denise*

But in your hearts set apart Christ as Lord. Always be prepared to give an answer to everyone who asks you to give the reason for the hope that you have. But do this with gentleness and respect.
1 PETER 3:15 NIV

Q&A

How can we as Christian girls speak up against the sins of this world? How can we witness to others with our actions and not be hypocritical?

First, by living out your convictions. For example, if you oppose certain movies, then don't go to them. If you know your friends are going to be drinking at a party, then don't go to that party. You can't force your convictions on others; that will only cause discord. Taking a stand against those things that disappoint God is a witness to others.

Second, one of the best ways to be a witness is to serve. Serving others is showing Jesus how much you love Him, not showing people how much you love Jesus. Third, being humble is a great exercise in avoiding hypocrisy. It's crucial to remember you, too, were once lost without Jesus. "Because all people have sinned, they have fallen short of God's glory" (Romans 3:23). A humble spirit will speak volumes to your friends who are watching Jesus being lived out in your life day by day.

—*Leigh*

[People can see] our purity, knowledge, patience, kindness, the Holy Spirit's presence [in our lives], our sincere love, truthfulness, and the presence of God's power.
2 CORINTHIANS 6:6–7

Q&A

I have a friend who gossips a lot, and I want to confront her and tell her that she needs to stop, but I'm afraid that we'll lose our friendship. How can I confront her without losing our friendship?

Keeping this friendship depends on how you approach your friend and how she chooses to respond to a gentle rebuke. It's wise to keep this issue to yourself until you decide what to do. If you start talking to other friends about the situation, then you're joining her game and you have no right to confront her. The book of Proverbs is full of verses about the tongue. Maybe you or you and your friend could do a Bible study on Proverbs.

Let God's Word guide you in finding the right time to talk about how hard it is for people to control their tongues. Maybe you can suggest you keep each other accountable for what you say. If this doesn't work, then you may need to gently confront your friend. Just be honest with her about the hurtful effects of gossip. She may not even be aware of how much she gossips. If she's a godly girl, then she will hopefully receive your words gracefully. If she doesn't, then you may need to distance yourself from her. Remember that if you're going to confront your friend on this issue, then you need to be upright yourself. Guard your tongue.

—*Heather*

O Lord, set a guard at my mouth.
Keep watch over the door of my lips.
Psalm 141:3

Q&A

What do you do when someone stinks, but you're afraid to tell the person?

This may seem like a funny question, but personal hygiene is a problem with lots of people, not just teenagers. There are two main things to consider here. First, how well do you know this person? If you are close to this individual (like a sister or best friend), then it's probably safe to say he or she would want you to speak up. You must be honest, but at the same time gentle and caring. This sort of "helpful yet hurtful" information will be hard for the person to receive, so tread carefully when choosing your words. However, in the end, the individual will be grateful for your honesty.

The second thing to consider is whether or not the smell is simply a personal hygiene problem (like not showering every day or not wearing deodorant), or if it's a medical problem. Some people, because of their hormonal makeup, may give off odors even if they've just showered that morning. If you suspect this is the case, you may want to see if a caring adult such as a school nurse can suggest the person visit a health practitioner to discover the root of the offensive odor.

—Shelley

*Everyone must live in harmony, be sympathetic,
love each other, have compassion, and be humble.*
1 PETER 3:8

Q&A

How can I still be nice to my friends when they're mean to me?

If they are truly your friends, they will care about your feelings. Maybe, just maybe, they haven't realized what they've done. You have to be honest with these friends. Speak the truth in love always (see Ephesians 4:15 NASB). The way these friends react will show whether or not they're your true friends.

If your friends aren't remorseful for the way they have treated you, then you may want to find some other people to hang out with. You must forgive your friends, but that doesn't say they have the right to be mean. You are to be kind, but it's OK to move on to people who see how great you are and want to be with you. I'm not saying this is an easy task. Pour your heart out to Jesus. He will be there to listen and to reassure you of your worth.

—Denise

Don't pay people back with evil for the evil they do to you. Focus your thoughts on those things that are considered noble.
ROMANS 12:17

Family

girls of grace

Q&A

It's so hard not to be angry with people, especially when their choices affect us. We all struggle with forgiveness at times. When I try to see people through their eyes, I'm often more sympathetic. For example, your mom and dad never married with the intention of getting a divorce. No matter the circumstances of the divorce, they are both hurting. I'm sure if asked, they would share how awful they feel because of the divorce's effect on you.

I'm so angry with my parents for breaking up our home! I know the Bible says I should forgive them, but I'm having a hard time. Help!

Forgiveness is a gift you give yourself. Harboring resentment will just make you more miserable. My husband comes from a broken home. He now wishes he had focused on his parents' love for him rather than holding on to anger for the many years he missed in getting to know his dad.

Forgiveness is not based on feelings, but a choice. You will most likely need to surrender your anger to God every day for a long time, but eventually your anger will fade. You don't have to agree with your parents' choices, but they are your parents and will always be your parents. We all need forgiveness in our lives. Thank goodness Jesus made the choice to forgive me.

—*Denise*

Put up with each other, and forgive each other if anyone has a complaint. Forgive as the Lord forgave you.
COLOSSIANS 3:13

Q&A

How do I get my mom to see my point of view?

Your point of view is very important. The best way to get anyone to hear your heart is to first speak in a kind and gentle tone. Proverbs 15:1 explains, "A gentle answer turns away rage, but a harsh word stirs up anger." When I communicate my viewpoint in anger, the results are confusion and nonresolution of the difference of opinion.

Second, be completely honest as you share your opinions and feelings. You desire to be clearly heard with an open heart and mind. You need to extend this same courtesy to your mom. She may understand your perspective, but it doesn't mean she will agree with it. Often we assume our way or opinion is the best way, but that is not necessarily true.

Lastly, apply these principles in hearing Mom's point of view, and maintain a teachable spirit. Working through differences can be particularly difficult because it may mean hearing and accepting another perspective, as well as diffusing other unresolved situations. Remember, parents don't claim to have all the answers, but the intention of their hearts is to do what they think is best for those they love and cherish.

—Leigh

A fool does not find joy in understanding but only in expressing his own opinion.
PROVERBS 18:2

Q&A

How do I respectfully obey my parents even though I disagree with their decision?

The key words in this question are "respectfully" and "obey." It was hard for me to always be respectful and obey my parents when I was a teenager. The Bible tells us in Exodus 20:12 to "honor your father and your mother," but it doesn't stop there. Ephesians 6:2–3 tells us that this is the "first commandment with a promise" (NASB). The rest of the passage says, "that it may be well with you, and that you may live long on the earth." In other words, there is a promise of blessing when we honor our parents.

I remember being so mad at my mom one day because she wouldn't let me go somewhere with my friends. She really didn't have a good reason for keeping me home; she just didn't let me go. I had to honor my mom, however, and respect her decision, as crazy as I thought it was. The funny thing was that Mom just wanted to spend some time with me. We ended up having a great time together. It's OK to respectfully disagree with your parents, but always remember that their decision is final and you must honor it.

—*Heather*

Children, obey your parents because you are Christians.
This is the right thing to do.
Ephesians 6:1

Q&A

First of all, please know you are not alone. Lots of kids grow up in households where they do not have Christian parents as positive role models. It is indeed hard to be in this situation. Your belief in Jesus and your decision to follow Him is most likely affecting the way you live your life, so I'm sure at times your choices are in direct opposition to those of your parents.

How do teens stay strong in Christ when they have unsaved parents?

Finding a strong Christian adult outside of your household to encourage you in building your relationship with Christ is something you need to do. Whether you talk with a teacher, neighbor, or even your youth minister, this person would be invaluable to you in the area of spiritual discipleship. Also, don't forget to go to God with the desires of your heart concerning your parents' salvation. He really does hear us when we pray with faith, even if it's just a little faith!

—Shelley

Desire God's pure word as newborn babies desire milk.
Then you will grow in your salvation.
1 PETER 2:2

Q&A

How can I deal with conflicts in my family?

Conflicts are always difficult. I avoid disagreements because they make me so uncomfortable. However, this is of little benefit in the long run. Communication is the key to resolving differences, and timing can be everything. You can't approach conflict when you are angry. Otherwise, you may say something that you don't mean. Ideally, it's always better if you have the opportunity to first pray about the troubling issue and make sure that your mind and spirit are open to honoring God.

Most conflict, however, happens in the heat of the moment and requires an immediate response. So take a deep breath, remember that there are always two sides to every disagreement, and ask God to give you a spirit of mercy. Obviously there are all types of conflicts from sharing the bathroom with your sister to dealing with major family secrets that aren't healthy for anyone. Some disputes may need someone on the outside to help mediate. Remember, sometimes it's OK to agree to disagree, but God always calls us to *love*. So carefully season your words with kindness and truth.

—Denise

So let's pursue those things which bring peace and which are good for each other.
Romans 14:19

Q&A

My dad has lived his entire life as a non-Christian. I try my hardest to make him believe, but he just gets mad. What should I do?

It's absolutely understandable that you would want your dad to embrace the saving knowledge of Jesus, but you can't put that enormous responsibility on yourself. "Indeed, the Son of Man has come to seek and to save people who are lost" (Luke 19:10). You have a responsibility to love and share Christ in the way *you* live and love Him. It's not your responsibility to change your dad's heart—that would be God's job. We are not responsible *for* God but *to* God.

My mother-in-law has been praying for her husband (my father-in-law) for more than twenty years. I know there have been times of defeat and disgust, but she has found peace in casting *all* her cares on the Lord, especially this one. We have to remember no one loves your father more than God, the One who beautifully designed your dad. Be encouraged, keep praying, and keep living as an example of Christ's freedom and redemption. The rest will happen in God's perfect timing.

—*Leigh*

The Lord isn't slow to do what he promised, as some people think. Rather, he is patient for your sake. He doesn't want to destroy anyone but wants all people to have an opportunity to turn to him and change the way they think and act.
2 PETER 3:9

Q&A

How can I encourage my family to walk the path of Jesus?

The greatest way you can encourage your family to be like Jesus is for you to strive to be like Jesus. This starts with you being consistent in your walk with Christ. Love your family even when they're being unlovable. Allow them to see how you respond to difficult situations in a godly manner.

Let your life be an example. You can't tell others to live a certain way if you aren't living that way yourself. Remember, it's not about your impressing your family with how godly *you* are. Instead, live a life that radiates the light of *Christ*, and this will glorify God and speak volumes to your loved ones.

—Heather

You are the light of the world. . . . Let your light shine before men in such a way that they may see your good works, and glorify your Father who is in heaven.
Matthew 5:14–16 NASB

Q&A

How can I be a good role model for my younger sister?

I love that you asked this question. Growing up, I had a sister eight years younger than I, and I treated her terribly. I have so many regrets now about what I did that I can at least tell you what *not* to do! You need to realize that even if your sister acts like she couldn't care less about you, she's truly watching everything you do and listening to everything you say.

Learn to treat your sister with kindness and respect. Sure, you will have your sisterly fights, but a gentle spirit can go a long way toward building a good relationship. Let your sister see you having your devotions and spending time with God. Offer to pray with her before she's about to do something important. Don't miss this beautiful opportunity to be a spiritual mentor to your sister, as well as a friend.

Invite your sister along with you and your friends every once in a while, just to show her that you value her and want to spend time with her. When you are older, you will be so glad that you even considered this question at your age. Trust me! I wish I had.

—Shelley

A servant of the Lord must not quarrel. Instead, he must be kind to everyone. He must be a good teacher. He must be willing to suffer wrong.
2 TIMOTHY 2:24

Q&A

My mom doesn't approve of some of the music I listen to. I don't really listen to the words. I just like the music. I know what the music artists are saying is wrong, and I won't do those things—so why can't I listen to that music?

In our book *Make It Real* Shelley discusses that "garbage in" is "garbage out." Philippians 4:8–9 says, "Keep your thoughts on whatever is right or deserves praise. . . . Then the God who gives this peace will be with you." God promises His peace when you attune your mind to things that are pure and worthy of honor.

You are kidding yourself to think that the lyrics you listen to do not affect your mind. I guarantee that when you hear the music, you know the words and probably sing along. When I eat junk food, it gradually affects my energy, the way I feel, and my figure. Listening to these lyrics will gradually affect you as well.

Also, whether we like it or not, God tells us to honor our parents. By honoring them, we honor the Lord. You honor your mom when you respect her advice about your music choices. You also need to consider your influence as a Christian young lady. When non-Christians see you listening to music that specifically goes against what you believe, don't you think that may be confusing to them?

—*Denise*

Brothers and sisters, keep your thoughts on whatever is right or deserves praise: things that are true, honorable, fair, pure, acceptable, or commendable.
PHILIPPIANS 4:8

Q&A

Several kids at school have credit cards and seem to buy anything they want. My parents won't give me a credit card, and I feel poor. How am I going to learn about handling money on my own?

You probably don't want to hear this, but your parents are actually doing you a favor. I honestly can't think of one good thing to say about credit cards. I know so many people who are in major debt because they simply misused their credit cards. When you get older, a debit card is really all you will need. It's sort of like a credit card, but it takes money that you actually possess out of your bank account, instead of allowing you to borrow money from a credit-card company and face a high interest rate in paying it back.

The way to learn about handling money on your own is to make your own money! Baby-sit, get a weekend job, do extra chores around the house. I promise you that when you make your own money rather than spend your parents', you will automatically become a better money manager. You are always more careful with what belongs to you. I also would recommend that you read a book called *Financial Peace* by Dave Ramsey. It's the best book I've ever seen on godly money management.

—*Shelley*

Do not weary yourself to gain wealth, cease from your consideration of it.
PROVERBS 23:4 NASB

Boyfriends and Love

girls of grace

Q&A

What do you do if you really like a guy, but he doesn't like you back?

It's disappointing when you realize that a guy does not share your interest and enthusiasm for a potential relationship. Trust me, this has happened to all of us at least once. But life is too short for you to consume yourself trying to win someone over. You are beautifully and wonderfully made, loved so much by your Creator (see Psalm 139:14 NASB). You have many attractive qualities, so don't be offended by those that may or may not find you attractive.

Be confident in who you are. The male gender is often attracted to girls who are self-confident. Not conceited, but confident. Seriously, don't strain yourself while trying to convince this person he should like you; instead, a mutual attraction should come naturally. You need to move on and remember that there are more "fish" in the sea.

—Leigh

I will give thanks to you because I have been so amazingly and miraculously made. Your works are miraculous, and my soul is fully aware of this.
PSALM 139:14

Q&A

Is it OK to have a non-Christian boyfriend?

No, it is not OK to date an unbeliever. A lot of girls are "missionary dating," thinking they can help bring their non-Christian boyfriends to the Lord, but the influence is often the other way around. In 2 Corinthians 6:14 God directs, "Do not be bound together with unbelievers; for what partnership have righteousness and lawlessness, or what fellowship has light with darkness?" (NASB).

If your boyfriend isn't a Christian, then he won't understand why you have high standards and why your faith in Christ is so important to you. Chances are you'll be pulled into his lifestyle and will lose your witness. Your number one standard for dating should be that your guy is a solid believer in Jesus Christ. Remember, every person you date is a potential candidate for marriage. Take this truth seriously.

I do think it's OK for you to have friends who aren't Christians; however, make sure those friends know you are a born-again Christian. Let these friends know where you stand on things, and limit extracurricular activities to mainly fun things you can do with them through your church.

—*Heather*

Stop forming inappropriate relationships with unbelievers. Can right and wrong be partners? Can light have anything in common with darkness? Can Christ agree with the devil? Can a believer share life with an unbeliever?
2 Corinthians 6:14–15

Q&A

My boyfriend says he's a Christian, but doesn't act like it. I don't have the guts to talk to him about it because I'm afraid he'll get mad. What should I do? I really like him.

The fact that you are discerning un-Christlike behavior in your boyfriend is a good sign. It means that the Holy Spirit is tapping you on the shoulder, reminding you that the company you keep can influence you when you least expect it. I hate to sound negative, but I think you shouldn't even be in a relationship with this boy if you can't talk to him about your faith and his too. You shouldn't have to fear your boyfriend's response about anything, especially when talking to him about something this important.

A true boyfriend-girlfriend relationship should be built on your common faith, not tiptoeing around it. I know it's hard to let go of someone when you really like him, but my advice would be to back away now. The longer you stay in the relationship, the harder it will be to end it. Remember, the Bible tells us we will know other believers by their fruit (see Luke 6:43–45). It doesn't sound like your boyfriend is bearing much fruit.

—Shelley

The fruit of the Spirit is love, joy, peace, patience, kindness, goodness, faithfulness, gentleness and self-control.
GALATIANS 5:22–23 NIV

Q&A

The guy I was dating broke up with me, and he broke my heart. I'm still trying to get over him. I don't like being this angry with him, and I've tried to let his memory pass, but it's hard. Can you give me some pointers?

A broken heart hurts so much, and for that I'm so sorry. It often takes time to heal deep wounds. It's OK that you aren't immediately over this loss. However, holding on to anger will eventually make your heart rot. Ephesians 4:31–32 direct us, "Get rid of your bitterness, hot tempers, anger, loud quarreling, cursing, and hatred. Be kind to each other, sympathetic, forgiving each other as God has forgiven you through Christ." Take your hurt and anger to Jesus *every* day!

Get yourself involved in something that causes you to think about someone else besides yourself. This boy just gave you the freedom to be everything God wants you to be. This guy would never have made you whole. No boy will! God has a purpose for you outside of any boy. Trust Him with your life. He will guide you, and eventually your pain will subside. I promise, because I've been there too.

—Denise

*The LORD is near to the brokenhearted
and saves those who are crushed in spirit.*
PSALM 34:18 NASB

Q&A

How important is it for my boyfriend to have a good relationship with his parents?

A good relationship is based on love and respect. If your boyfriend does not love or respect his parents, that is cause for alarm. The Bible tells us in Ephesians 6:1–2: "Children, obey your parents in the Lord. . . . Honor your father and mother" (NASB). There is a difference, however, between honoring and obeying. As children, we are to be obedient to our parents as long as we are not being disobedient to God. Understand?

Honoring our parents is showing respect and love toward them for a lifetime. This is not an option, but a command by God. As long as your boyfriend is relating to his parents with thoughtfulness, respect, and love, he does have a good relationship with them. And, yes, that is very important! If your boyfriend is showing a lifetime of respect toward his parents, chances are he will do the same to you. Otherwise, you can expect trouble in your relationship.

—Leigh

Honor your father and mother. Love your neighbor as you love yourself.
MATTHEW 19:19

Q&A

How do you get over a guy you know God doesn't want for you?

I'm proud of you for recognizing that this guy is not the person God has for you. I also commend you for obeying God and ending the relationship. I believe that God will reward your faithfulness and obedience to Him, and He will heal your wounded heart.

The best way to get through this breakup is to spend time in the Word and prayer. As you begin to look at the situation from God's perspective (the Bible), things will gradually make sense and you'll see hope on the horizon. Waiting for God's best in relationships isn't always fun, but it is worth it. I can say this because I didn't meet my husband until I was twenty-eight years old.

At times I despaired, wondering if God would ever provide a godly man. Yet in my waiting, God taught me a lot about myself and to really trust in Him. One day you will look back and thank God for taking you through this tough time because He taught you to depend on Him and to believe that He does know what's best for you in every circumstance. Who knows, Mr. Right may be just around the corner.

—Heather

Wait with hope for the LORD. Be strong, and let your heart be courageous. Yes, wait with hope for the LORD.
PSALM 27:14

Q&A

How do you know if your boyfriend loves you for you and not just for the physical?

First, eliminate the physical and see if your boyfriend hangs around. Other signs to observe are whether he wants to know about you, your interests, hobbies, etc., and wants the best for you, whatever that may be. When he talks to you, do you feel like you are the only one in the room?

Is he comfortable hanging out with both you and other friends together? If your boyfriend loves you for who you are, he won't just always want to be with you alone. Perhaps most importantly, your guy will want you to love Jesus more than he wants you to love him.

— Denise

You were bought for a price.
So bring glory to God in the way you use your body.
1 CORINTHIANS 6:20

Q&A

How do you know when you're in love with someone?

When love is not based on an emotion but based on 1 Corinthians 13:4–7: "Love is patient, love is kind. It does not envy, it does not boast, it is not proud. It is not rude, it is not self-seeking, it is not easily angered, it keeps no record of wrongs. Love does not delight in evil but rejoices with the truth. It always protects, always trusts, always hopes, always perseveres" (NIV). This definition is the best rule of thumb by which to measure love.

By following God's description of love, you can separate your emotions from what is real. It's so easy to get caught up in the heart-throbbing moment and equate that feeling to "being in love." But love is not a feeling; it's a lifetime commitment of taking the good with the bad and accepting them both.

—*Leigh*

My dear children, let's not just talk about love; let's practice real love.
1 JOHN 3:18 MSG

Q&A

How do you know a guy loves you—really *loves* you?

In the Bible we read about three types of love. The Greek word for brotherly love is *phileo*. The Greek *eros* means sensual love, and *agape* is unconditional love. True love has an aspect of all three. True love says that a guy loves you because you are his fellow human and he wants what is best for you (*phileo*). True love is also physically attracted to you (*eros*). Most importantly, true love is unconditional (*agape*).

Agape is love with no strings attached and even loves when you are unlovable. This love makes you more important than self and models a willingness to even die for you. *Agape* is the love that God has for us and that He displayed by sending His beloved Son to die for our sins. Because we're sinful, our love for one another is flawed and will in no way be perfect like God's love for us, but we're to strive to live out God's love in our relationships. Because you are a treasure, don't settle for any guy that does not seek to follow the example of God's true love.

—*Heather*

This is love: not that we have loved God, but that he loved us and sent his Son to be the payment for our sins. Dear friends, if this is the way God loved us, we must also love each other.
1 JOHN 4:10–11

Sex

Q & A with Point of Grace · Sex · Q & A with Point of

girls of grace

Q&A

I've had sex before marriage, and I feel like I'm not worthy of marrying someone who is a Christian virgin, even though that's what I want. I feel like I've ruined God's plans for my future spouse. What can I do?

Growing up I often felt the same way, but I am living proof that it's *not* true. God is not going to punish your spouse because of your choices. Have you truly repented of your sin? If you have, then "the old way of living has disappeared. A new way of living has come into existence" (2 Corinthians 5:17). My friend, you are a new creature in Christ! This means the abundant life that Christ promises is yours (see John 10:10). So don't let the Enemy tell you otherwise.

Our God is a forgiving God, and His mercies are new every morning. He also wants you to forgive yourself. If you struggle with guilt over your actions, God wants you to know that He does not condemn you and neither should you. "So those who are believers in Christ Jesus can no longer be condemned" (Romans 8:1).

You asked what you could do. I strongly suggest that you live your life loving and serving God with all your heart, soul, and mind. Stay close to Him and trust the hope-filled plans He has for you.

—Leigh

I know the plans that I have for you, declares the LORD. *They are plans for peace and not disaster, plans to give you a future filled with hope.*
JEREMIAH 29:11

Q&A

I know that sex before marriage is wrong and kissing is OK. So how far is too far to go with your boyfriend?

First of all, who said that kissing is necessarily OK? I don't want to sound like a prude, but a kiss can be a very intimate thing. It's difficult to kiss intimately without wanting to go further. Girls are so moved by emotion. When a girl really kisses someone, she begins to give her heart away to that person. Scripture directs you in Proverbs 4:23 to "guard your heart." For a girl, that's really hard to do once she kisses a guy. And a guy is even more easily turned on. When he starts kissing you, he can't help but want to go further.

It feels good to have a boy desire you. I know that from experience, but true love means you think of the other person and not just yourself. If you truly love a guy, then you will want the very best for him— including helping him guard his passions so they honor God. It's not your responsibility to be the keeper of your boyfriend's heart and mind, but you can help him by not putting him in a situation that causes him to stumble. It is, however, your responsibility to keep your own mind and heart pure.

—Denise

There isn't any temptation that you have experienced which is unusual for humans. God, who faithfully keeps his promises, will not allow you to be tempted beyond your power to resist. But when you are tempted, he will also give you the ability to endure the temptation as your way of escape.

1 CORINTHIANS 10:13

Q&A

Kids in school think that oral sex is OK because it's not the same as intercourse. What should I say to them?

Well, the kids in school are wrong. Why else would it be called oral *sex* if it weren't sex? This kind of sex is becoming rampant in our schools today, and it's just as wrong as having intercourse before marriage. We always get asked the question: how do you know if you are going too far with a guy? If you have to ask that question, then you are probably going too far.

The ultimate reason you are to abstain from such sexual acts is that your body is to glorify God. God designed sex to bring honor to Him only in a marriage relationship between a man and woman. Outside of marriage any kind of sex is a sin. FYI: you can get sexually transmitted diseases by having oral sex too.

—Heather

It is God's will that you keep away from sexual sin as a mark of your devotion to him.
1 THESSALONIANS 4:3

Q&A

Is it wrong to mess around with a guy who's just a friend? (By "mess around," I mean sexual activities.) You know—"friends with benefits."

Let me make it really simple for you. It's wrong to "mess around" with a guy—period. The fact that you are asking about being physically intimate with "just a friend" cheapens the true intent of love and sex even more. Commonly called "hooking up," this superficial practice is completely contrary to God's plan for sex and sexual activities.

Sex is sacred, only to be shared between husband and wife. Sexual intimacy is not some casual activity to engage in the same way you would go shopping or to a movie. Sex is a serious gift from God. Your body is yours and God's alone until your wedding day when you say, "I do." Then and only then is engaging in sex or sexual activities OK.

—*Shelley*

The body is not for sexual sin but for the Lord, and the Lord is for the body.
1 CORINTHIANS 6:13

Q&A

Is phone sex OK?

Absolutely not. God did not create the beautiful union of sex so His creations could belittle it through lewd language and seductive fantasies. Sex is only for marriage between a man and a woman. It's as simple as that. To try to arouse someone with your words over the telephone (or through computer "cybersex") is causing lust that God warns us about in both our hearts and minds. People communicating lustful thoughts and words via phone are creating false intimacy in the relationship. Phone sex is never OK, and godly teenagers should take a stand against it.

—*Shelley*

Don't let sexual sin, perversion of any kind, or greed even be mentioned among you. This is not appropriate behavior for God's holy people.
EPHESIANS 5:3

Q&A

If your boyfriend pushes you to do things you're not comfortable with romantically, should you keep going with him if you're in love with him?

No. If you have told your boyfriend your boundaries and he continues to push, then he doesn't truly love you. Obviously your boundaries should be set at a level that does not take your boyfriend mentally and physically to a point where it's hard for him to turn back. If you stop all physical contact, I would be surprised if the boy stays around if all he's looking for is physical intimacy. You deserve someone to want what's best for you.

When you aren't comfortable in a situation, that is the Holy Spirit letting you know the situation is not right. I know it's hard, but you need to let this guy go. God specifically directs us in 1 Corinthians 6:18 to "stay away from sexual sins" because it harms our own bodies.

—*Denise*

Stay away from sexual sins. Other sins that people commit don't affect their bodies the same way sexual sins do. People who sin sexually sin against their own bodies.
1 CORINTHIANS 6:18

Q&A

If you're in love with a guy and plan to be with him forever, is it wrong to have sex with him?

Absolutely! God's design for marriage offers so many wonderful things, and one of them is the element of surprise when it comes to sex. Sex between a husband and wife is protected by marriage. Lovemaking is the most intimate time between a husband and wife. And until the marriage covenant has taken place, sexual intimacy is not an option.

Sex outside of marriage is treated as a physical act, yet within marriage, sex is an act of commitment to one another. Within marriage, sex can be a relationship builder. Outside of marriage, sex can be destructive. Why not choose to begin your marriage the best way possible—God's way.

—*Leigh*

Stay away from lusts which tempt young people.
Pursue what has God's approval.
2 TIMOTHY 2:22

Q&A

A couple of my very close girlfriends are having sex with each other. I've always been taught that this is wrong, but now I'm beginning to wonder. Some advice, please?

I want my words to be full of grace, but I have to say—same-gender sex is always wrong and grieves the heart of God. God designed sex as a wonderful experience between a man and woman within the boundary of marriage. Outside of marriage, sex is immoral and dangerous. Unfortunately, as young people's bodies and sexual feelings blossom, some fall into inappropriate sexual experimentation.

It is crucial that your friends stop their behavior, and they may need to talk with a Christian counselor. Your friends' sexual choices must be disheartening to you, but don't let their actions distort the picture of God's true intentions for sex. God wants to restore these girls to sexual wholeness, so love and pray for your friends, and point them to God's healing truth.

—Heather

Let us behave properly as in the day, not in carousing and drunkenness, not in sexual promiscuity and sensuality, not in strife and jealousy. But put on the Lord Jesus Christ, and make no provision for the flesh in regard to its lusts.
ROMANS 13:13–14 NASB

Q&A

In this case, you should simply trust your heart, your own "deep down." What's wrong is wrong, and your conscience is telling you that, so take heed. I'm pretty sure you don't want a guy who cares more about the "bad girls" and what they can do for him, than he cares for a nice girl like you. Hold out for a guy that you need do nothing more for than be yourself. He will respect you for *you* and your purity.

—*Shelley*

I feel like I am supposed to be like the "bad girls" to get the guys—but deep down, I know that's wrong. What should I do?

Dear friends, now we are God's children. . . . So all people who have this confidence in Christ keep themselves pure, as Christ is pure.
1 JOHN 3:2–3

Faith

Q&A

I feel like I'm steadily decreasing in my walk with God. I try and try, but somehow I keep slipping away. How can I get back to God?

I love that you asked this question. We forget that we are responsible for our own spiritual nurturing. The challenge is to spend time with God every single day the rest of your life. I'm not talking about a "quiet time" where you lock yourself in a closet with your Bible for two hours. I'm referring to a basic element of living your life with God—prayer. Every day, you can pray—while taking a shower, driving to school, whatever and whenever. Prayer seeks God, letting Him know you need Him in your life.

After you pray spend a few quiet moments letting God speak to your heart. Then I encourage you as often as you can to study God's Word. I wrote this down many years ago: "Read God's Word to obey it, not to understand it." Finally, I encourage you to abide in the vine (see John 15:5). Author Cynthia Heald explains in her book *Abiding in Christ,* "Abiding is consistently sitting at the feet of Jesus listening to His words with a heart to obey." If you take these steps, I promise you will revive your friendship with God.

—*Leigh*

You who seek God, let your heart revive.
PSALM 69:32 NASB

Q&A

I want to find time for Bible study, but I can't. What advice do you have?

You *can* make time, though you may need to get up earlier or go to bed a little later. It's a cop-out to say you can't find the time. We all make time for what's most important in our lives. If you daily spend two or three hours watching TV, talking on the phone, or surfing the Internet, don't tell me you don't have time to meet with God.

Honestly, I've never had a hard time studying the Bible until I had children. I, too, have to check my priorities. Occasionally, my husband and I like to unwind from a long day by watching a little TV or a movie. However, sometimes I haven't spent time with the Lord yet, and I have to make a choice between God and TV. There is only one right choice, but even at my age sometimes the choice is difficult.

Keep asking yourself what is most important. What is going to help you make better choices in your Christian life? Psalm 119:9 says, "How can a young person keep his life pure? [He can do it] by holding on to your word." The only way that you can be more like Jesus is to be in God's Word.

—Heather

I want to reflect on your guiding principles and study your ways.
PSALM 119:15

Q&A

How can I know for sure that I'm going to heaven when I die?

Being assured that you'll go to heaven is basically simple. God made the gospel so easy that even small children can understand it. If you believe in your heart that Jesus Christ is the Son of God and that He died to pay the penalty for your sins, and you accept His gift of forgiveness for your sins, then you will be saved. Romans 10:9 says, "If you declare that Jesus is Lord, and believe that God brought him back to life, you will be saved."

Saved from what? Saved from eternal hell, which is reserved for those who never trusted in Jesus. Heaven is real and is our inheritance when we choose Christ. Once you've turned to Jesus for eternal life, it's important to profess your faith and to join in fellowship with other Christians.

If you've made a commitment to follow God, but still doubt at times that you'll go to heaven, you need to understand that these doubts are a tool of the Enemy to confuse you. As a Christ-follower, you are now a part of God's forever family, and He will never turn His back on you.

—Shelley

This is the testimony: God has given us eternal life, and this life is found in his Son. The person who has the Son has this life. The person who doesn't have the Son of God doesn't have this life.
1 JOHN 5:11–12

Q&A

How do you know when to forgive someone?

I usually know that I need to forgive someone when I can't get my mind off how this person has wronged me. I can tell that I need to forgive when I'm starting to harbor resentment. We are always supposed to forgive. The Bible talks about forgiving "seventy times seven" (Matthew 18:22). We always have to remember that Christ has forgiven us.

Forgiving is a choice. I heard a speaker once say, "When you forgive, it takes the offense away from you." Forgiving lets people off the hook from your wrath. Let God be God, and let Him be the judge. Not you.

—Denise

The LORD is merciful, compassionate, patient, and always ready to forgive.
PSALM 145:8

Q&A

What can I do to feel complete with God and not depend on a guy for happiness?

People may bring us happiness, but only God can complete us. God designed life that way. Your relationship with God is not based on a feeling, but on a personal relationship with His Son, Jesus Christ. As a result, Christ will never leave you nor forsake you. This is a promise from God. Happiness is based on momentary circumstances, but joy comes from God. In God's presence there "is fullness of joy" (Psalm 16:11 NASB).

So get in the presence of God. "Draw near to God and He will draw near to you" (James 4:8 NASB). Spend time with Him as often as possible—read, study His Word, and pray. I leave you with the words of Jesus Himself. "Until now you have not asked for anything in my name. Ask and you will receive, and your joy will be complete" (John 16:24 NIV).

—Leigh

I will find joy in the LORD. I will delight in my God.
ISAIAH 61:10

Q&A

I have done some really bad stuff in my past. What can I do other than ask for forgiveness?

Asking for forgiveness is a wonderful idea, but you also need a repentant heart that desires to turn away from sin. Nobody is perfect. We all have "stuff" for which we are not proud. One of God's amazing attributes is His forgiveness. However, you must keep a short account with God regarding your sin. If you don't, before you know it, you'll have buried a sin you didn't confess and for which you didn't receive His forgiveness.

Once you confess and repent of sin before God, you then must accept His forgiveness. You can rest in God's precious promise in 1 John 1:9: "If we confess our sins, He is faithful and righteous to forgive us our sins and to cleanse us from all unrighteousness" (NASB). When you offer your sins with a sincere heart to God, He completely cleanses you. Don't wallow in your past failures or guilt; walk in freedom. In Isaiah 43:25 God declares, "I alone am the one who is going to wipe away your rebellious actions for my own sake. I will not remember your sins [anymore]."

—Heather

Put your hope in the LORD, because with the LORD there is mercy and with him there is unlimited forgiveness.
PSALM 130:7

69

Q&A

How do you manage to stay a good Christian with all the evil there is around us these days?

Evil is essentially Satan's destructive forces that are immoral or wrong, and they do pervade our world. Unfortunately, evil comes at us from all sides, especially through media that increasingly flaunts sex and violence to get our attention. As Christians we have a job to be *in* the world, spreading God's love, but not *of* the world. There has to come a point where our faith convictions set in and we *separate* ourselves from the sin around us. This, however, will not always be the easy road.

To "stay a good Christian," you can try practical things like avoiding questionable movies and TV shows—even if your friends watch them. If things you know are immoral are going on around you, you should try your best simply to stay away from them. Remember, just because we're Christians doesn't mean we won't have temptations. But always cling to this truth: "The one who is in you is greater than the one who is in the world" (1 John 4:4).

—*Shelley*

The fear of the Lord is wisdom!
To stay away from evil is understanding.
JOB 28:28

Q&A

OK, here's the skinny: some bad stuff happened to me, and I was mad at God for a while. Was it wrong to have been mad at God? And to sometimes still be mad at Him?

God knows everything you think and feel. Also, although it may be difficult to grasp, nothing has ever happened that did not first go through God's hands. So God can handle your anger, and it's OK to ask Him, "Why?" God is not offended by your questions. You do have to understand, however, that He is God, and His "ways are higher than [our] ways" (Isaiah 55:9). We have a song that says, "Who am I to try and solve the mysteries behind heart and soul of all that I believe?"

God knows every detail of the bad stuff you experienced. These things may not seem fair or good, but God still has a good plan for you. Your personal story has a purpose, even though you may not fully understand that purpose right now. Psalm 33:4 explains, "everything he does is trustworthy." You essentially have to trust God or your feelings.

The problem with being mad is that you put up a wall that hinders relationships, and staying mad does nothing for anyone. Communicate. Tell God how you feel. When you do, you'll start a deeper relationship with Him, deeper than you ever thought could exist.

— Denise

Trust in Him at all times, O people; pour out your heart before Him;
God is a refuge for us.
PSALM 62:8 NASB

71

Q&A

What do you do if you sometimes feel like God isn't helping you or you don't feel loved by God?

I have to remind myself of what I mentioned before: having a relationship with God is not based on your feelings. It's based on a relationship with Jesus. Once you have a relationship with Jesus, His love for you will *never* go away, no matter your circumstances. Once you recognize that, you will realize that those troubled feelings are not coming from God but from Satan. The Enemy wants you to believe that God could not love you as much as He does. If Satan can convince you of that, he has won.

The Bible states in Nahum 1:7, "The LORD is good, a refuge in times of trouble. He cares for those who trust in him" (NIV). Psalm 46:1 explains, "God is our refuge and strength, an ever-present help in times of trouble." These are only two of God's many promises to His children. Why would God want to jeopardize His reputation on us if He didn't truly love us?

—Leigh

I love you with an everlasting love.
So I will continue to show you my kindness.
JEREMIAH 31:3

Q&A

How do you control your attitude?

This can be a really tough thing to do, especially as a teenager. I remember being sixteen and thinking that I was the only one who really knew anything. I thought that I could make decisions for myself better than anyone else. However, I had very wise parents who didn't allow me to get too big for my britches.

It's good to have one or two people in your life who keep you accountable. Not just about what happens on your dates, but accountable about how you are treating your parents or siblings or even your teachers for that matter. My mom still calls me on the carpet sometimes. It still hurts when I hear that she thinks I might need an attitude adjustment, but when I step back from the situation, I always know that she's right.

Ask yourself this: does my attitude exemplify the fruit of the Spirit? Your life is to reflect the fruit of love, joy, peace, patience, kindness, goodness, faithfulness, gentleness, and self-control (see Galatians 5:22–23). If these qualities are not evident in your attitude and actions, then you may need to do some adjusting.

— Heather

Don't act out of selfish ambition or be conceited. Instead, humbly think of others as being better than yourselves. Don't be concerned only about your own interests, but also be concerned about the interests of others.
PHILIPPIANS 2:3–4

Q&A

What is the best way to stay close to God and build a personal relationship with Him? And why is this so hard?

The best way we can know God is through His Word. It's really the only tangible thing we have that is directly inspired by God Himself. By spending time reading the Bible and memorizing Scripture, we can know God's personality better. And the better you know someone, the closer your relationship becomes.

Another way to stay close to God is to simply talk to Him. God wants you to converse with Him whenever you can. He already knows what's going on in your life, so why not talk to Him about it? You can do this not only when praying, but also at other times, such as while driving in the car or doing a chore.

I think the reason it's so hard to keep your relationship fresh is because so many other things can easily captivate and distract you. Life is full of activity! If you're having trouble finding time to keep your relationship with God strong, it's probably a good indication that you're simply too busy. To make time with God a priority, something from your life most likely needs to go.

—Shelley

Let Christ's word with all its wisdom and richness live in you. Use psalms, hymns, and spiritual songs to teach and instruct yourselves about [God's] kindness. Sing to God in your hearts.
COLOSSIANS 3:16

Q&A

How did you balance academics and your relationship with God?

I'm probably not the best one to answer this because academics was not my thing. But I do realize that teenagers today are bombarded with homework and activities. It's hard to fit everything in. I also realize how vital it is to nurture your relationship with God. Remember that you can talk to Him anywhere—running laps in track, driving to school, taking a shower.

Interacting with God is truly a choice. Get up five to ten minutes early to read a small devotion. Put a Scripture up in your locker to meditate upon for the week. If you have time to e-mail friends or talk on the phone, you have time to talk to God! Believe me, I am speaking to myself as well. God doesn't expect an hour-long Bible study every day. He just wants to be a part of your every moment.

—*Denise*

Search for the LORD and his strength. Always seek his presence.
1 CHRONICLES 16:11

Q&A

How can God answer or listen to so many prayers at once? I know He hears all our prayers, but can He really *answer* them all at once?

First of all, God does not answer prayers with an instantaneous hocus-pocus act. God is omnipresent, or in existence everywhere at once, and He is omniscient, knowing everything. Because God is both omnipresent and omniscient, He can be all things at all times.

Since God is the creator of time, He answers our prayers in *His* perfect time. God may not answer our requests "overnight"; instead, He perfectly plans out the details of His responses to fit His overall purpose. Our tiny minds struggle to understand the enormous power and provision of God, but the truth is, He can do anything!

—*Leigh*

Almighty LORD, you made heaven and earth by your great strength and powerful arm. Nothing is too hard for you.
JEREMIAH 32:17

Q&A

I know I'm saved and all, but my relationship with God is not strong anymore. I don't feel I have much faith. Please help!

Have you ever expressed words similar to the psalmist's: "How long, O LORD? Will You hide Yourself forever?" (89:46 NASB). "Do not hide Your face from me in the day of my distress" (102:2 NASB). Have you cried out to God, wondering where He is? Perhaps you have experienced His presence, but now you don't sense Him anywhere in your life. If so, then you are like the writers of the Psalms. The Psalms reflect the cries of ones longing to be in God's presence and securely trust Him.

You are not alone in questioning the strength of your faith. Sometimes God allows us to go through seasons of testing, and our belief can feel weak. If you are a born-again believer, then rest assured that God will "not fail you or forsake you" (Joshua 1:5 NASB).

Sin can also hinder your faith. Psalm 139:23–24 says, "Search me, O God, and know my heart; try me and know my anxious thoughts; and see if there be any hurtful way in me" (NASB). Be sure to bring your sin or hurtful ways to God. Honestly communicating with God will help get you back on track spiritually and will renew your faith day by day.

—Heather

God, who shows you his kindness and who has called you through Christ Jesus to his eternal glory, will restore you, strengthen you, make you strong, and support you.
1 PETER 5:10

Q&A

I know God has called me into His service, and I believe He has something special for me, but how do I know what it is?

We are all called to live lives of service to God if we are believers, but I'm assuming you are speaking specifically about being called into some sort of special ministry. If you know in your heart you have been called to something like this, it's only a matter of time before God will reveal this ministry to you.

It is your job, in the meantime, to be faithful to Him in the little things of your life, and when obvious opportunities present themselves, you have to remember that God speaks through circumstances. God will, in His time, bring about the exact circumstance that will determine your future calling.

—Shelley

Everything has its own time,
and there is a specific time for every activity under heaven.
ECCLESIASTES 3:1

Q&A

I have the desire to minister to teen girls, but how can I get everything organized, planned out, and actually put into action? What advice do you have for me based on your experience with Girls of Grace?

It all starts with prayer. I'm not an organizer either, so we found someone who had that gift to help pull things together. You'll never feel like you are fully ready, but at some point you just have to jump on in. Before you roll out any plans, research to understand a little more the needs of teenage girls.

Once you step out, just be there for the girls more than anything. It can be simple things like taking them to lunch once a month for a start. Or find a Bible study to do together. Girls thrive on relationships. Develop your friendships first, then move on into more of the issues. Love on these girls—that's what they need more than anything.

—*Denise*

Love each other with a warm love that comes from the heart.
After all, you have purified yourselves by obeying the truth.
As a result you have a sincere love for each other.
1 PETER 1:22

Q&A

If God already knows everything, why is it important to pray?

Prayer is not for God's benefit but for our benefit. Speaker Ross Winker says, "Prayer is a conversation between two people who love each other." God desires to hear from us and for us to listen to Him. You can't have a relationship without communication. Praying is our way of communicating with God.

When we repent of our sins, we come prayerfully to God for forgiveness. When we pray we seek God's help and acknowledge our need for Him in our lives. The Bible invites us to pray (see Hebrews 4:16), and Jesus often modeled how to pray. He even prayed during His final moments on the cross!

It's important to remember that prayer is not just about asking, but also about thanking and praising God. Prayer is also our opportunity to hear the voice of God. "But in everything, by prayer and petition, with thanksgiving, present your requests to God. And the peace of God, which transcends all understanding, will guard your hearts and your minds in Christ Jesus" (Philippians 4:6–7 NIV).

—*Leigh*

Pray in the Spirit in every situation. Use every kind of prayer and request there is. For the same reason be alert. Use every kind of effort and make every kind of request for all of God's people.
EPHESIANS 6:18

Q&A

How can you know you've been forgiven of your sins?

First of all, you have to ask yourself if you really trust and believe that what God says in His Word is true. If you don't believe what the Bible says, then you will always doubt that you've been forgiven. God is, by His nature, forgiving. Acts 10:43 says, "People who believe in the one named Jesus receive forgiveness for their sins through him."

The Bible is also clear that "God is faithful and reliable. If we confess our sins, he forgives them and cleanses us from everything we've done wrong" (1 John 1:9). Therefore, we have to confess our sin, then repent or turn from our sin, and receive forgiveness. Receiving is the hardest part. But if you trust God's Word, then you must receive the forgiveness He offers.

— Heather

I, even I, am he who blots out your transgressions,
for my own sake, and remembers your sins no more.
ISAIAH 43:25 NIV

Q&A

Who do you listen to or go to for answers when you come to a gray area in your life that isn't directly talked about in the Bible?

I think the very best "person" to listen to in this situation is the Holy Spirit. If you are a believer, the Holy Spirit lives in you. The Holy Spirit usually comes in the form of a still, small voice inside of you, whispering to your spirit whether what you are about to do is right or wrong. God's promptings are undeniable, but whether or not you listen is up to you.

God knows what is best for you, and you can choose to ignore the voice (some people might refer to this as their conscience) or follow the lead of the Holy Spirit when making decisions. As a general rule of thumb, though, if the area seems gray to you, it's probably best to steer clear and use caution. The fact that you recognize a questionable area may be a signal in and of itself that something is not quite right.

—Shelley

The helper, the Holy Spirit, whom the Father will send in my name, will teach you everything. He will remind you of everything that I have ever told you.
JOHN 14:26

Q&A

How can you tell what God's will is for you and what He wants you to do with your life?

Determining God's will is a step-by-step process. Bible teacher Henry Blackaby, in his workbook *Experiencing God*, says to look at what God is doing around you and join Him in it. Psalm 119:105 says, "Your word is a lamp for my feet and a light for my path." God promises to light your path, and you can't move a step without His notice. God will also lead you through circumstances and other people.

We are people who want to see the whole picture now, but it's the day-by-day path that takes us on our journey. When you feel called to do something, you will have peace about it, even if it's not easy to do. His Spirit will continue to speak things to your heart, but you've got to take quiet moments to hear from God. If you work on giving your best to God in all you do, He'll be the one to take you where you need to go.

—Denise

You watch me when I travel and when I rest.
You are familiar with all my ways.
PSALM 139:3

Q&A

Can I still be a Christian and be sad sometimes? I'm trying to trust God, but happiness sometimes seems far away.

Absolutely! The Bible shares story after story about downhearted people. Abraham loved God but was sad because he wanted children. Throughout much of the book of Psalms, David cried out to God during times of deep despair. Paul suffered with sadness, too, while trying to convince those he loved to stay faithful.

Everyone will experience sadness whether he or she is a Christian or not. But we know as Christians that our sufferings have a purpose. We also have to remember that happiness is based on our circumstances. As a result, we will not always be happy, and that is totally normal.

Paul encouraged the Philippians to not let their circumstance dictate their inner attitudes. Philippians 4:4 reminds us, "Always be joyful in the Lord! I'll say it again: Be joyful!" Your ultimate joy comes from a relationship with Jesus and knowing that no matter what, Jesus is always with you.

—*Leigh*

But let all who take refuge in you rejoice. Let them sing with joy forever. Protect them, and let those who love your name triumph in you.
PSALM 5:11

84

Q&A

What do I do if I used to be into church, but now don't know whether or not I believe in God anymore?

This is a really big question. I wish I knew why you are questioning your belief in God. But let's start by recognizing that the church is the body of Christ, not some building that you visit. If you are a born-again believer in Jesus Christ, then you have a responsibility within the body of Christ to use your spiritual gifts in a local body (church). A human body won't be at its best if it's missing a body part; neither will the body of Christ. Your church and my church need us to bring our spiritual gifts so that our churches can function to bring God glory. Look at 1 Corinthians 12.

Now, I went through a time in my life when I questioned God's ways. I never questioned, however, whether I believed in Him. Here is what concerns me: there is a difference between believing intellectually and truly putting your trust in Jesus Christ and His painful yet glorious death on the cross as the payment for your sin debt to God. James 2:19 says that even the demons believe there is a God. Look deeply into your heart. I pray that you will see that Jesus really is the way, the truth, and the life.

—*Heather*

Jesus answered him, "I am the way, the truth, and the life. No one goes to the Father except through me."
JOHN 14:6

Q&A

When you choose to live for God, how can you still follow Him when you're in school or around people who don't believe?

You have to be strong, especially if you are a new Christian. Ask God every day before school to help you have the strength to honor your choice to follow Him. Also, equipping yourself with God's Word in your heart will really help you. When things start to get tough at school and you feel like throwing in the towel and going along with those who don't believe, it is beneficial to recall helpful verses from the Bible.

Finding close Christian friends, especially someone at your school, will also encourage you in the tough times. Always remember that the choice you have made to live for God is an eternal one, and what your school and friends thought about that choice will one day not matter at all, but your relationship with God is forever.

—*Shelley*

Receive your power from the Lord and from his mighty strength.
Put on all the armor that God supplies.
In this way you can take a stand against the devil's strategies.
Ephesians 6:10–11

Q&A

How do you know when you're saved?

You can't know if you are saved by just your feelings. At some point in your life you realized that you needed God. You believed that His Son, Jesus, came to this earth for all of us because we had all been wrong in the eyes of God. Jesus was perfect and never sinned.

He died on a cross as a penalty for all the mistakes you have made and will ever make. By saying to Jesus, "Please forgive me, be my Savior. I give my life to You," you are asking Jesus to take the place of your sins, and now you are perfect in God's eyes. You are saved. That will never change. Now, go on and live for Him!

—Denise

We were dead because of our failures, but he made us alive together with Christ. (It is God's kindness that saved you.)
Ephesians 2:5

Point of Grace
Close Up

girls of grace

Q&A

How is it that *every* time you walk on stage, you're so happy and full of energy? Don't you ever just have a bad day—even when you have a concert or conference?

Bad days are inevitable whether you have a concert or not. Life continues to have high and lows for each one of us. Honestly, one of the benefits of having four members is that when one is going through a rough time, we can rally around the one hurting. It truly is a blessing to be surrounded by godly women.

One of our responsibilities as "professionals" is to perform with excellence. That means putting on a happy face even when we're feeling low. I'm not saying that we're being fake, but sometimes, like you, we have to stay focused in spite of our emotions. When we have a job to do, yet we're too weak, we trust God to be our strength. God is so great at this when we are not.

—Leigh

I can do everything through Christ who strengthens me.
PHILIPPIANS 4:13

90

Q&A

What is your favorite Point of Grace song?

I have always loved the song "The Great Divide." To me, it's one of the most powerful songs ever written about the gospel. So many people have told us how God used this song to help them really understand the good news. Our society doesn't like to talk about sin, and some people don't even believe they are sinners. Well, I am a sinner, and the greatest news that I could ever hear is that God made a way whereby He could maintain His holiness, bring about justice, and still save sinners. "He made Him who knew no sin to be sin on our behalf, so that we might become the righteousness of God in Him" (2 Corinthians 5:21 NASB).

The gospel is our eternal hope, and Jesus is the only bridge we have to God. "The Great Divide" paints a marvelous picture of what Jesus did for us. The songwriters actually mistyped the original lyrics "there's a bridge to cross the great divide" to read "a cross to bridge the great divide." But they realized these words are just as powerful, and I agree.

—*Heather*

Christ died for us while we were still sinners.
This demonstrates God's love for us.
ROMANS 5:8

91

Q&A

How do you stay close to God when you're on the road and so busy?

Actually, staying close to God on the road is not as difficult as it might seem. On the road we have fewer things to distract us, and our focus is mainly on the concerts. So we have more time in the day to read our Bibles and dwell on the things that God may be trying to teach us. Also, when our children aren't with us (they are about half the time), we have lots of quiet time in our hotel rooms to pray and talk to God.

Home life is much harder, however. We're just like most other moms, struggling to find a balance among all the demands. At home every day is different, and schedules get crazy just dealing with things around the house and with work. So with all the chaos, it's definitely harder to be still and make time for God. Strangely, though, it's in the chaotic times that we all need Him the most.

—shelley

Since you were brought back to life with Christ,
focus on the things that are above—where Christ holds the highest position.
Keep your mind on things above, not on worldly things.
COLOSSIANS 3:1–2

Q&A

How did you guys first start out? Were you kids with a dream? Did you know somebody who could get you a record deal? How did it happen?

We were in college together at Ouachita Baptist University. We decided one night in a dorm room that we were going to make a group and go sing at youth camps and churches for the summer. Never would we have dreamed that this could be our career. After that summer people kept calling us to come sing.

About two years later we went to a music competition in Estes Park, Colorado. There we met John Mays, who was at the time an executive for Word Records. John liked what we were doing and asked us to sing a demo for the record company. They liked us and asked us to sign a deal with their company. We've been with Word Records ever since.

—*Denise*

A person may plan his own journey, but the LORD directs his steps.
Proverbs 16:9

Q&A

What are your favorite foods?

Reduced-fat sour cream Pringles, chips and salsa, and chicken fajitas from Garcia's restaurant. Plus, anything my mom makes: cubed steak, black-eyed peas, macaroni pie, and rice and gravy. My favorite desserts are chocolate cream pie and the NutRageous candy bar. I love food!

—*Leigh*

Who can eat or enjoy themselves without God?
ECCLESIASTES 2:25

Q&A

Do any of you still struggle with self-esteem issues?

In some ways we'll always face questioning our self-image. Our world tells us we have to look a certain way, do a certain job, or maintain a certain status. Magazines, movies, and TV shows don't help us feel good about ourselves. On TV's extreme-makeover shows, we see people's amazing outward changes and may wish for those kinds of changes for ourselves. But these surface changes only make people feel good temporarily. We all leave the mirror and have to deal with how we feel on the inside. To this day I still struggle with the way I look. Shelley deals daily with body-image issues, Denise with comparing herself to others, and Leigh with measuring up to everyone else's expectations.

Girls, as Christians our esteem cannot come from the outside. Our confidence and our esteem come from Christ in us. We are not only made in the image of God, we *are* the image of God. With the world's pressures, we all at times may wobble in our self-image, but ultimately, our esteem is in the One who made us just the way we are. We are all called to be stewards of what God has given us, both on the inside and outside.

— Heather

God created humans in his image. In the image of God he created them. He created them male and female.
GENESIS 1:27

Q&A

In your experiences, did you feel God calling you to do what you do, or did you just decide to use the gifts God gave you?

I think it's probably different for each of us, but for me, I think both happened. I first decided to use my voice to sing just Christian music instead of any other kind of music. Then we formed Point of Grace in college, and before I knew it, I did sense a true "calling." Our music efforts evolved from a singing group to a ministry right before our eyes.

If you are faithful to use whatever your gifts or talents are for the glory of God, He will reveal to you your true calling in life. Someone once told us "it's not a ministry until someone else calls it a ministry." This means that you shouldn't label yourself as a minister; rather, your ministry develops as you simply serve others.

—*Shelley*

We always pray that our God will make you worthy of his call. We also pray that through [his] power he will help you accomplish every good desire and help you do everything your faith produces.
2 THESSALONIANS 1:11

Q&A

How do your children and husbands feel about you traveling?

Our husbands are truly incredible. God knew what each of us needed in a spouse. Our husbands have been so supportive through the years and have willingly carried a lot of the load. Our kids love our tour bus. "The Bus" is the coolest thing in the world to them. Now that we all have so many kids, they can't come as often as we would like.

My boys are old enough that they will ask sometimes why Mommy has to go sing all the time, but they seem to understand. As long as my kids get to travel with us once in a while, they're fine to be at home with Dad the rest of the time.

— *Denise*

Husbands, in the same way be considerate as you live with your wives.
1 PETER 3:7 NIV

Q&A

How and where did you meet?

I actually met the girls when they were called Say So many moons ago. Then in 1994 my husband and I moved to Nashville to continue our musical careers. Years later, Point of Grace asked my husband, Dana, to play guitar in their band. Dana eventually became the group's music director, while I continued my own singing career.

During those years we became good friends with the girls and their families. I actually subbed for Terry a time or two. When Terry retired I was asked to join the Point of Grace family. The rest is history. I love sharing the stage with these great women and having them in my life as dear friends.

—Leigh

See how good and pleasant it is when brothers and sisters live together in harmony!
PSALM 133:1

Q&A

What is your main goal in life?

I want to be Christlike. In my marriage, as a mom, in my church, and in my ministry, I want to react and respond the way Jesus would. I am far from this, but I am hoping that as each day goes by, I'm becoming a little more like Him. I have days and sometimes weeks that set me back, but the goal is still the same. I know I was made in the image of Christ, my goal in life is to reflect that reality.

Finally, I desperately want my kids to love God with all their hearts, souls, minds, and strength. I want them to be good stewards of the gifts God has given them. Most of this responsibility falls to my husband and me to lead by example. If our kids see Mommy reading the Bible every day, then they'll hopefully make this a part of their lives as well.

The apostle Paul said, "Imitate me as I imitate Christ" (1 Corinthians 11:1). This is so hard, but I pray for my kids every day that they will be so compelled to love God and serve Him with their lives. That is the greatest legacy I could ever leave.

—*Heather*

One thing I do: forgetting what lies behind and reaching forward to what lies ahead, I press on toward the goal for the prize of the upward call of God in Christ Jesus.
PHILIPPIANS 3:13–14 NASB

Q&A

Other than the Bible, what is the most powerful book you've ever read?

I actually enjoyed the Mitford series by Jan Karon. These fiction books are about a small-town Episcopal priest who pours himself into the lives of others. Through reading these books, I've learned so much about how to really savor relationships and how to treat others well.

This series has also changed my perspective on what is important in our chaotic and busy lives. Every time I pick up one of these books, I'm reminded to "stop and smell the roses." This is the only life that we have on earth, and if people don't matter, then what is the point? I have often yearned to live in Mitford!

—Shelley

Do for other people everything you want them to do for you.
LUKE 6:31

Q&A

What is the scariest thing that has happened on your tours that makes you either laugh now or marvel at God's protection?

During the first four years of our singing career, we drove around in a van and trailer probably twenty days a month. Every night we would take two-hour shifts to drive. We were so young and clueless! God protected us mightily during those years. In thinking back I marvel that we had maybe three breakdowns the whole time. In our last trip in our old van, we broke down on the highway about four hours outside of Nashville. It was dark and scary with no exits anywhere close. Back then we didn't even have cell phones.

Our engine was smoking and looked like it was going to burst into flames. However, it never did. A highway patrolman finally stopped and took us to a truck stop where I called my husband to drive from Nashville to get us. That was the last time we used that van. Our manager made us buy a brand-new one, which we were afraid we couldn't afford. But about six months later we paid the van off. When we sold that van, we were finally blessed to be in a bus that someone else could drive.

—Denise

The LORD will watch over your coming and going both now and forevermore.
PSALM 121:8 NIV

Q&A

Were all of you friends before you started singing?

Most of us, yes. Heather and I have been friends since the fourth grade. Then Heather and I became friends with Shelley in college. Through our relationship with our great guitar player, Dana Cappillino, we met Leigh. Our group was definitely based on friendship before music, although it's music that ties us together. I have the best job in the world. I get to sing about Jesus, travel, and meet wonderful people—all with friends that I love so much.

—*Denise*

As Christians, do you have any encouragement? Do you have any comfort from love? Do you have any spiritual relationships? Do you have any sympathy and compassion? Then fill me with joy by having the same attitude and the same love, living in harmony, and keeping one purpose in mind.

PHILIPPIANS 2:1–2

Q&A

What's your favorite song?

This is an impossible question to answer because there are way too many songs to narrow it down to one. However, I do have a favorite songwriter, and that is Nichole Nordeman. I have loved every song she has written. She writes such thoughtful lyrics, very deep but understandable at the same time. Nichole's song "Every Season" is a masterpiece; I am in awe of anyone who can pen such a beautiful song. I guess I have great respect for talented songwriters because I don't have that gift. I wish I did.

—Heather

He placed a new song in my mouth, a song of praise to our God. Many will see this and worship. They will trust the LORD.
PSALM 40:3

Q&A

Where did you get the name "Point of Grace"?

John Mays is a wonderful man who "discovered" us and signed us to our record deal. When we moved to Nashville before we made our first record, we were called Say So. But there was another group at the time with the same name, so we had to change ours.

John, along with several other people, submitted a list of names for us to consider. John had been reading a C. S. Lewis book and came across the phrase "we live everyday at the point of God's grace" and jotted these words down on his list. For some reason, the phrase popped out at us. It seemed very fitting for where we were at that time and also where we wanted to continue to live—at the point of God's grace, needing Him for everything and completely dependent on His grace to save us. So we all agreed and finally had a name that fit us just perfectly.

—*Shelley*

Let us draw near with confidence to the throne of grace,
so that we may receive mercy and find grace to help in time of need.
HEBREWS 4:16 NASB

Q&A

Were you all virgins when you got married?

I am so glad you asked this question. I just wish I could answer "yes" like the rest of the group. I regretfully admit I made some bad choices in my dating relationships. The pressure that I put on myself to be like the "rest of the world" was not worth it! Although I cannot go back and change the mistakes of my past, I hope to use those experiences to help young girls like you avoid "suffering the consequences." Trust me, there are consequences.

Some outcomes of premarital sex are damaging physically, like sexually transmitted diseases. Some are damaging emotionally, like shame and guilt—which can be just as deadly. I struggled for over ten years in a losing battle with shame and guilt. God reassures in 1 John 1:9: "If we confess our sins, He is faithful and righteous to forgive us our sins and to cleanse us from all unrighteousness" (NASB). Although I "knew" Christ had forgiven me of my sins, it wasn't until I believed this in my heart that I gained freedom and liberty to move on. Girls, life is too short to give up Christ's freedom and liberty for a life of shame and guilt.

—*Leigh*

Keep yourself morally pure.
1 TIMOTHY 5:22

Q&A

What guidelines do you follow when selecting clothing for onstage performances?

We hire a professional clothing consultant to shop for us. Before she begins shopping, we give her very specific guidelines and inform her of our individual preferences. Some may like long jackets versus short ones. Some may prefer skirts to pants. Some may like bright colors versus pastels. We try to be as specific as possible. Because each one of us has a different body type, our consultant helps ensure that the right outfit is the most becoming on each individual.

Our biggest request is to get clothing that represents modesty with a very hip look. For example, when we wear low-rise jeans, we wear tanks underneath tops so that we are "covered" when we bend over. They also come in handy when a top is too low cut or see through. Tanks provide a great service—coverage instead of skin.

We've also learned that wearing things too tight can make us look bigger—you'd be surprised what trying the larger size can do for your figure. We don't go by sizes anymore; we go by the fit.

—Leigh

A person who listens to advice is wise.
PROVERBS 12:15

Q&A

Who is your hero and why?

At this point in my life, I view every mom as my hero. She may work outside the home or stay at home. She may be a single parent or married, rich or poor—it doesn't matter. Every mom that strives to raise her children to be godly young people and strives to manage an organized household is my hero.

Ultimately, my own mom is my hero. I call her Mamma. She was and is the queen of our family and her efficient home. I've watched her daily spend time with God and live out her love for the Lord. As my sister and I grew up, our mom was not perfect, but she could be honest about her imperfections.

I can talk to my mother about literally anything, and I trust her wise counsel because she is intimate with God. She is still my mamma, but even more now she is a dear friend. I've heard that you know you were a good mother if your daughter grows up wanting to be a mother. I always wanted to be a mother, and now that I am, I know that I want to be just like my mamma.

—Heather

A good name is more desirable than great wealth.
Respect is better than silver or gold.
PROVERBS 22:1

Q&A

Which quote or phrase do you consider to be your motto?

I don't always practice this, but it's surely my goal to "live every day as if it were your last." I am reminded in a song that we sing called "This Day" that God does not promise us tomorrow. We do, however, have a precious gift called Today for us to live life fully and love others well.

I hope to live life with as few regrets as possible and hopefully use the bad times and bad decisions as learning experiences. I think it's so important to look at every day positively, embracing all our experiences, from the exciting to the mundane as gifts from God to enjoy.

—Shelley

You don't know what will happen tomorrow. What is life?
You are a mist that is seen for a moment and then disappears.
JAMES 4:14

Makeup, Fashion, and Body Image

Q&A

I'm clueless when it comes to putting wardrobe pieces together. Can you give some general guidelines to help me?

Honestly, I'm pretty clueless too. Here are a few things I try to do. Grab the latest *InStyle* magazine or other fashion magazines and look at what is trendy. Go to the mall and window-shop. Most stores have a designer that arranges the latest styles. Notice the pieces that stand out. Take note and try to apply the styles and colors to the clothes you have. Think about your current wardrobe to see if you have any of those pieces.

Everyone can use a few classic pieces in her closet: a great pair of jeans, a white button-down shirt, a fun jacket, a great pair of shoes. A stylist on a photo shoot once told me that things don't have to be "matchy matchy" anymore. Start with some of your favorite clothes and work around those pieces. Not every piece you're wearing has to be outstanding, but pick one thing that adds a little zing to make an outfit special. It might just be the accessories.

—*Denise*

Stop worrying about what you will eat, drink, or wear.
Isn't life more than food and the body more than clothes?
MATTHEW 6:25

Q&A

How old should I be to wear makeup?

I think I was in sixth or seventh grade when my parents gave me permission to wear makeup. Although, looking back at old pictures, I wished they had prevented me from wearing makeup until high school. I looked hideous—way too much makeup for such a young face! I wore a clownlike combination of bright blue eye shadow and dark red lipstick. Fortunately, makeup application has come a long way since I was a teenager. The rule now is "less is more." This is a great advantage for us parents.

Thirteen or fourteen is probably the earliest age I would recommend wearing makeup, especially when considering daily usage. I suggest doing what I eventually plan to do with my daughter. With the permission of a parent or guardian, go to a makeup counter at a mall department store (e.g., Clinique or MAC) and ask the professional to suggest makeup colors as well as teach application. The makeup consultant is trained to consider skin type, eye color, and age appropriateness. This will save you time and probably money. Wearing makeup can be so much fun. To quote my mom, "Makeup should enhance your beauty, not cover it up!"

—*Leigh*

A wise person will listen and continue to learn, and an understanding person will gain direction.
PROVERBS 1:5

Q&A

One of the many things that I love about God is that He is so creative. Just look at the world. What if we all looked and dressed alike? How boring. God made you with a distinctive look and personality. You are "fearfully and wonderfully made" (Psalm 139:14 NIV), and you are called to be a good steward of the body God gave you.

I'm not really into makeup or "cute" clothes, but some people seem to look down on me for this. What do you think?

Embrace whatever it is that makes you feel beautiful and feminine. Maybe it's a nice smelling perfume or a certain outfit. You don't have to wear makeup to fit in. Although, being the makeup fanatic that I am, you never know how a little bit of mascara and lip gloss can brighten your face. It's crazy for someone to look down on another person for not looking or dressing a certain way.

—Heather

God does not see as humans see. Humans look at outward appearances, but the LORD looks into the heart.
1 SAMUEL 16:7

Q&A

How can I be cute and fun but still modest?

Most girls want to dress cute and stylish, but let's face it—it's hard these days to be cute, stylish, *and* portray a godly image. These features don't exactly go hand in hand. It infuriates me when I go shopping for a simple shirt and everything I try on is skintight! Not to mention the low-cut jeans and short, short skirts. You could get a complex about your body from a simple shopping trip.

The good news is that with a little thought and resourcefulness you *can* look fun and modest. If shirts are too short, wear a bodysuit underneath so your stomach doesn't show. Shirt too low cut? No problem, simply wear a cute tank underneath. Skirt too short? Just don't buy it. Opt for pants or look for a longer skirt instead, or try the skirt over a pair of jeans. Sweaters too clingy? Try jackets or blazers instead.

I've also found it helpful to just ignore sizes and buy what fits, not what size I wish I were. For instance, I used to wear an 8, but 8s aren't what they used to be! So now I buy a 10 or a 12, and a better fit is always more modest and flattering.

—Shelley

I want women to show their beauty by dressing in appropriate clothes that are modest and respectable. Their beauty will be shown by what they do, not by their hair styles or the gold jewelry, pearls, or expensive clothes they wear.

1 TIMOTHY 2:9

Q&A

So many girls my age strive to be supermodel thin. I keep beating myself up for being a little overweight. What does a "healthy body image" really mean?

A healthy body image comes from seeing yourself as the very image of God. We were created in His image. Our lives and our actual beings reflect Him. We are His creation, and as John Calvin once said, "creation is the theater of God's glory." God also created us with brains to make good choices to be healthy. We should be stewards of the bodies God has given us. We should eat right and exercise because it's what's best for our bodies and gives us strength. Plus, balanced nutrition and exercise make you feel so much better!

I always dread going to the gym, but afterward I'm in the best mood. As far as trying to be model thin, that's striving after an empty goal. Glamorized pictures of models are not reality. You definitely need to adjust your perspective. I've struggled with my weight all my life. I've lost and gained many times, and honestly, I always feel better when I'm at a healthy weight for my body—but not skinny. And when I am at my best weight, it's because I'm eating right and exercising. Don't compare yourself to others. You are a one-of-a-kind creation of the highly creative God.

—*Heather*

Bring everyone who is called by my name,
whom I created for my glory, whom I formed and made.
Isaiah 43:7

114

Emotions and More

Q&A

How do you deal with your friends being depressed and trying to help them without getting depressed yourself?

For an occasional period of depression, like sadness over a breakup with a boyfriend, be a shoulder for your friends to lean on. Be understanding, but encourage your friends to press on. Depression over a death or depression with a medical cause, however, may require more healing time. Don't assume you need "answers" for every situation; just be there to listen. Romans 12:15 says, "Mourn with those who mourn" (NIV). If a friend is seriously depressed, encourage him or her to get professional help (a pastor, Christian counselor, or doctor). Getting help is a sign of strength, not weakness.

Be careful not to compromise your own needs to meet the needs and protect the feelings of your friends. This is codependency and not a great foundation for friendship. (*Please Don't Say You Need Me* by professional counselor Jan Silvious is a great book about maintaining healthy relationships.) Don't base your response to your friends on *their* unsettled emotions. Instead, love your friends through their difficult times, and pray for God to give them strength and wisdom. Show support, but your friends need to do the hard work to get better. In all this, trust God to heal your friends' emotions.

—*Leigh*

In their distress they cried out to the LORD.
He rescued them from their troubles.
PSALM 107:6

Q&A

How can you gain more confidence in yourself?

You have to see yourself as an amazing creation of Almighty God. God Himself created you and loves you with an everlasting love. One of my favorite Bible passages is Isaiah 43:1–4 where God still loves the children of Israel even though they are obstinate and disobedient. God says, "Do not be afraid, because I have reclaimed you. I have called you by name; you are mine. . . . You are precious to me, you are honored and I love you." We can apply these endearing words to our lives and know that God adores us.

The psalmist knows God's love well when he declares in Psalm 139 that he is "amazingly and miraculously made." I love verses 17 and 18: "How precious are your thoughts concerning me, O God! How vast in number they are! If I try to count them, there would be more of them than there are grains of sand." Notice the exclamation points in these verses. David is confident in how God views him.

When you're feeling down and you've lost your confidence, read about God's love for you in His Word. Don't measure yourself in human eyes; instead, dwell on how God sees you and be confident!

—*Heather*

Look! God is my Savior. I am confident and unafraid, because the LORD is my strength and my song. He is my Savior.
ISAIAH 12:2

Q&A

How do you deal with stress?

I don't know that I have one particular way, but I'll try to give you a few tips that have worked for me. Being prepared before the stressful situation begins can help a lot. For instance, if you have studied hard for a test, your stress level will automatically be less than if you hadn't prepared. So, thinking ahead is my first advice.

Second, I love to consider the verse in Philippians 4:6, "Be anxious for nothing, but in everything by prayer and supplication with thanksgiving let your requests be made known to God" (NASB). "Be anxious for nothing" means "don't stress out." Put things in perspective when you're in a stressful situation. After all, we have the Creator of the universe on our side, so how bad can things really be?

Internalize the knowledge that you already have and make it real—that God Himself hears you, is with you, and will not leave you. Hopefully this will bring peace to most any stressful situation.

—Shelley

*When I worried about many things,
your assuring words soothed my soul.*
PSALM 94:19

Q&A

What does the Bible say about a person hurting herself (such as: cutting yourself, burning yourself, etc.)?

God tells us in 1 Corinthians 6:19–20, "Don't you know that your body is a temple that belongs to the Holy Spirit? The Holy Spirit, whom you received from God, lives in you. You don't belong to yourselves. You were bought for a price. So bring glory to God in the way you use your body." God's Word also tells us that we are made in the image of God. Do we really think God wants us to hurt our bodies? We are His children! I have two boys, and I'm so sad when they get hurt.

The act of cutting or hurting oneself stems from a need to relieve a much deeper pain. Self-cutting is just a temporary numbing of the real pain, and the person will eventually need more and more drastic means to keep the real wound from being exposed.

If you are injuring yourself, find someone to help you work through your real pain. This is a serious issue, and only God can be the true healer. He wants to get rid of your pain altogether. Cutting and hurting yourself is self-destructive. Remember, God has great plans for your life. Hurting yourself is not part of them.

—*Denise*

I am suffering and in pain. Let your saving power protect me, O God.
Psalm 69:29

119

Q&A

What would be the best advice you could give to assure someone that anything is better than giving up?

I think you have answered the question yourself: don't give up! Anyone can give up, but it takes a strong person to finish the race. Romans 5:3–5 says, "We also rejoice in our sufferings, because we know that suffering produces perseverance; perseverance, character; and character, hope. And hope does *not* disappoint us" (NIV, emphasis mine). No one said the Christian life is easy; it is accompanied by sorrows and pain. But we are reminded through this scripture that our suffering is not meaningless; the outcome of suffering is a part of God's purpose in our lives.

It has been said that if we didn't experience sorrow, we could not appreciate joy. And if we don't have pain, we can't experience God's healing. In my experience, it was in my brokenness that I finally yielded to God's way instead of my own. I did not give up on life but rather gave God the broken pieces of my life; then He put them back together with the help of my friends' love and encouragement. What the devil means for harm, God will use for the good.

—Leigh

Since we are surrounded by so many examples [of faith], we must get rid of everything that slows us down, especially sin that distracts us. We must run the race that lies ahead of us and never give up.
HEBREWS 12:1

A with Point of Grace · Difficult Issues · Q
th Point of Grace · Difficult Issues · Q & A w
race · Difficult Issues · Q & A with Point of
icult Issues · Q & A with Point of Grace · D
es · Q & A with Point of Grace · Difficult Is
A with Point of Grace · Difficult Issues · Q &
nt of Grace · Difficult Issues Q & A with Poi
ce · Difficult Issues Q & A with Point of G
icu Issues Q & A with Point of Grace · Di
es · Q & A with Point of Grace · Difficult Is

Difficult Issues

We asked our dear friend Nancy Alcorn, founder and president of Mercy Ministries, along with the counseling staff at Mercy to share their sensitive and wise counsel in addressing the following issues. Nancy has worked with troubled youth since 1973, and Mercy Ministries provides free residential care, biblical counsel, and life-skills training for hurting teen girls and young women. We are honored to help Nancy and Mercy Ministries bring healing and hope to thousands of wounded girls and their families every year through speaking about them everywhere we do concerts. It's our privilege to share the incredible results we have seen through this ministry with others, that they might get involved in prayerfully and financially supporting their ministry along with us.

girls of grace

Q&A

What do you do when someone tells you she wants to kill herself?

You will want to get her help as soon as possible. Listen to this person and reassure her there are other ways to deal with her pain. Pray with her and share scriptures that describe God's desire for her to live out her full potential. Ask if she has a specific plan of suicide. If she does, you will need to call the local suicide hotline or police department.

If you're with your friend, wait with her until help arrives (unless your own life is threatened, in which case you should leave immediately). If your friend does not have a suicide plan, try to gain a verbal and/or written agreement that she will not hurt herself. Immediately contact a counselor or health professional to assist your friend.

God is with you, and He will guide you in the words to say. As a support person, do not try to take on the role of savior in this individual's life. Only Jesus can be her Savior, but you can be a vessel God uses to guide her to caring, professional help to lead her onward. Continue to pray for this person as she works through her journey to wholeness.

He will rescue the needy person who cries for help and the oppressed person who has no one's help.
PSALM 72:12

Q&A

I think I'm pregnant. I feel empty and lost and don't know what to do. Can you please help me?

First, know that God still loves you and has a plan for you and your baby (see Jeremiah 29:11). That plan may be for you to parent or it may be for you to give a wonderful gift to a couple that wants to adopt. Don't make any hasty decisions (like abortion). Abortion is not a quick fix and will lead to years of sorrow and regret.

It may not seem like it right now, but you do have options. Unplanned pregnancy brings a flood of emotions. Denial, shame, and guilt may cause you to withdraw from God and others. It may be scary to tell someone, but carrying a secret alone will weigh you down.

Find supportive, pro-life people to help you (parents, family members, church friends, counselor, crisis pregnancy center, or a program like Mercy Ministries). If you're not yet ready to tell your parents, the supportive help you find can assist you in telling your family. Your family and loved ones may require time to process your pregnancy news, but don't give up. Continue to call on the support of the other resources mentioned above. There is always help available to encourage you in your decision to give life to this child.

Peace I leave with you; My peace I give to you; not as the world gives do I give to you. Do not let your heart be troubled, nor let it be fearful.
JOHN 14:27 NASB

Q&A

Please give any advice you can for girls growing up in homes of divorce.

The most important thing for you to know is that the divorce was not your fault. This was something that happened between your parents, but their decision is affecting you. It's OK for you to love both of your parents. You do not have to pick one of them to love more than the other.

For right now, be open and honest with your parents about what you want and need. For instance, talk to your parents if you feel they're trying to get you to play favorites or use you as a messenger so they can avoid each other. Or let them know if you're unhappy about your living or visiting arrangements. Try to come up with a realistic plan for a solution that everyone can agree on.

Be cautious about trying to manipulate one parent against the other, because this will only damage your long-term relationships with them. Remember that God is not the author of your pain. Living with divorced parents may be difficult, but God will strengthen you if you trust in Him. You may want to consider talking with a pastor, counselor, or teacher for support during this time.

Speak the truth to each other.
EPHESIANS 4:25

124

Q&A

I'm around friends who cut every day. I've already cut three times, and I'm scared I'll do it again. What do I do?

You and your friends are not alone in your struggle. The increasing pressures on young people today, including grades, dating relationships, and abusive home situations, leave many teens uncertain about how to handle the emotions that come with the pressure. Cutting often occurs when anger is stuffed or suppressed. When buried feelings surface, people turn to self-harm to release the painful feelings. But the sense of relief is only temporary, which is why the behavior usually continues until it becomes a habit. Self-harm may also include scraping, biting, hitting, or pulling hair.

Healthier options for dealing with your emotions exist. Give yourself permission to feel angry, then express your anger to God. Journaling or taking a walk often helps too. You also might need to separate yourself from your friends who cut until they've dealt with their own problems.

If you feel you cannot stop yourself by using the resources mentioned here, you need to let someone you trust know right now that you're in danger of hurting yourself. Don't be ashamed. Remember, what is hidden in secret will have power over you. Get help and give God a chance to bring you peace.

Let go of anger, and leave rage behind.
PSALM 37:8

Q&A

I know God can help with stuff, like eating disorders, cutting, etc. But how can I get rid of the pain that comes after?

Sometimes, when God has taken care of the "stuff," He still needs time to deal with the root issues that brought the "stuff" into your life in the first place. Just as with physical pain, emotional pain draws attention to a wound or hurt in your life. Because many emotional wounds are not usually visible, it's easy to try to ignore the pain. But the emotional pain alerts you that something inside you needs attention and care. Pain is like a neon sign pointing to the place in your heart that needs the healing touch of God.

As you surrender your pain to God, there are a few practical steps you can take. The healthy way of dealing with pain is to find godly counsel, continue to read your Bible, participate in praise and worship, and get connected in a church. These areas will give you needed support and encouragement to work through your pain. Remember, though, that pain is a part of life, as are peace, love, joy, and hope. The God of the universe is on your side. He wants to come into your life to heal the pain of your wounded heart completely.

Relieve my troubled heart, and bring me out of my distress.
PSALM 25:17

Q&A

I have this friend who keeps trying to kill herself. I want to help and tell her about Jesus, but I'm afraid she won't want to be my friend anymore. What should I do?

The risk of rejection is always present when sharing the gospel with others, but if your friend never hears about Jesus, you run an even bigger risk of losing her. As a true friend, be willing to place the welfare of your friend and her receiving truth above the friendship itself. Given time, she will understand and appreciate your actions.

Perhaps you could share your concerns with her by saying, "I really care about you and about our friendship. Seeing you hurt in this way hurts me as well. I want to make things better for you, but I know I can't possibly fix everything. There is Someone I know, however, who has brought peace and joy into my life and is always there for me when I'm going through hard times. I'd love for you to know Him too."

The responsibility to change your friend's behavior rests upon her, but you can point her to the One who is able to free her of torment. Extend the hope that you have found in Christ. Nothing is worth more than that. (To know how to respond if your friend is serious about suicide, please refer to page 122.)

We felt so strongly about you that we were determined to share with you not only the Good News of God but also our lives. That's how dear you were to us!
1 THESSALONIANS 2:8

Q&A

Is abortion wrong if the pregnancy would kill the mother?

This is a controversial issue even among many Christians. Facing this dilemma must be a heart-wrenching situation for any expectant mother (and father). Someone in this position may find help in knowing that God is the author of life, and He considers each person's life precious in His hands.

In the case of an extreme medical emergency, there is no blanket answer. Prayer and seeking God's guidance are crucial to discerning the Holy Spirit's leading in each individual case.

There are stories of mothers who chose to leave things in God's hands, and they and their babies survived labor and delivery. Other women sacrificed their own lives so that their children might live, while still others made the very difficult decision to preserve their own lives.

In all these situations, we can rest assured that God is faithful to lead and guide us through even the darkest circumstances. God's truth remains: He will be an ever-present help in time of need.

If any of you needs wisdom to know what you should do,
you should ask God, and he will give it to you.
God is generous to everyone and doesn't find fault with them.
JAMES 1:5

Q&A

If someone you love has sexually abused you, should you tell anyone?

You need to know absolutely that the abuse is not your fault. Your mistreatment breaks God's heart, and He wants to heal you of all your physical, emotional, and spiritual wounds. Telling someone about abuse can be quite scary. The devil wants you to fear the "what ifs" if you expose the abuse. Shame can also keep you from speaking up. The devil torments through secrets. He wants you to think you should protect the abusive loved one and that it's not loving if you tell.

But by exposing the abuse, you will do three things. The abusive loved one can get appropriate help, the abuse you've suffered will stop, and you might protect someone else from this person's abuse. It is never easy to reveal a shameful secret, but the truth can help end the abuse.

Don't wait. Talk right away to a trusted authority—a parent, teacher, friend's parent, or counselor. If the first adult you talk to does not get you help, then go to another adult until you find someone who will listen and help. Trust God and believe that He will guide you and protect you when you reveal the abuse. There is help, hope, and healing for you!

Heal me, O LORD, and I will be healed. Rescue me, and I will be rescued. You are the one I praise.
JEREMIAH 17:14

Q&A

What do you do when someone you know is bulimic or anorexic?

Approach her, and if necessary, confront her in love. Let her know that you know and you want to help. Just telling her that she is not fat and/or critiquing what she eats will not be helpful. This individual's distorted perception of herself will not change until she deals with the root of the problem. Find out how willing she is to change her behavior. This can be hard, because if she is not ready to get help, you cannot force her.

If this person's parents do not know, ask her if you can help her tell her parents or someone else who can help, like a counselor, pastor, or teacher. If she tries to blow off her food habits or make it sound like her eating issues are not a big problem, don't fall for it. Eating disorders are very serious, and they don't just go away on their own.

Be careful not to take on the responsibility to make this person change. For change to happen, she has to want to change. Your role is to direct her to help and support her in the process. Pray for the Holy Spirit to work on her heart.

You will know the truth, and the truth will set you free.
JOHN 8:32

Q&A

Life is not making sense to me. I'm thinking about suicide because God doesn't really appeal to me, and nothing my friends say helps. Can you help me?

Yes! There is an answer for your pain and a reason to live. Until you can process the root cause of your desperation, you may have to first *choose* to live. Suicide is not the answer. What you seek is meaning in your life, not the end of your life. Even if you are not interested, God still loves you. God wants to free you from your depression, hopelessness, and despondency so that you might live life fully, not just exist.

You have at least some hope within you; otherwise, you wouldn't have asked this question. Deep down you believe that things can be different without taking your life. It may be hard right now to hang on to a glimmer of hope, but please don't keep your despair to yourself.

You need to talk to someone other than a friend—a caring adult such as a parent, teacher, or health professional. Don't assume people know you are suicidal, and don't wait to go to them because you think they *should* know. People can't read your mind or actions. You have to tell someone specifically what you're struggling with so he or she can help you. Talk to this person today!

The thief comes only to steal and kill and destroy;
I have come that they may have life, and have it to the full.
JOHN 10:10 NIV

Q&A

Whatever you do, do not give up on God! You must come to a place where your faith in God does not depend on what you see, especially in your father's life. God is at work even when what you see does not seem to be changing.

My dad is an alcoholic, and I pray and pray that God will heal him of this disease. How do I keep from getting discouraged and losing my faith in God?

Alcoholism often begins with the need to drown an unresolved hurt or emotional wound. In my opinion, alcoholism is not a disease such as cancer or diabetes, but rather a destructive habit that starts with a choice to use alcohol to avoid life or numb pain. God is willing to take care of the hurts that people sometime drown in alcohol; however, they must choose to let God work in their lives.

Some people simply choose not to believe God can deal with their hurts, or maybe they don't know that God can do that. No matter what your dad's situation is, don't stop offering consistent prayers for him. God is willing and able to soften your father's heart if your father is open to Him; He is also able to carry you through this difficult season. Keep reflecting the light of Christ into your dad's life, and remember that your Father in heaven is always with you.

Let us not lose heart in doing good,
for in due time we will reap if we do not grow weary.
GALATIANS 6:9 NASB

Q&A

My father gave me up for adoption. I've never even seen him, but I feel lonely without him, and I don't know if he loves me or not. How can I get past this empty feeling inside?

Sometimes out of necessity or duress, a father makes the tough decision to allow someone else to raise his child. Often this decision is based out of love more than out of dislike or burden. Your father most likely made what he thought was the best decision at that time—to put you into the hands of a loving family.

It's normal for a girl to crave a relationship with her father. The emptiness you feel could be feelings of abandonment or worthlessness. Letting God fill the hole in your heart will be key to your healing. You cannot change your father's decisions of the past, but you can let your heavenly Father change your future. You can let the past dictate your present living, or you can make a choice to move beyond it.

When you enter into a relationship with Jesus Christ, He adopts you into His family. God's Word is full of His promises to be faithful to you. God wants to heal every single pain you have about the loss of your father. Seek counsel from a pastor or counselor to help you work through the healing process. You really can find freedom and peace over your adoption.

Even if my father and mother abandon me, the LORD will take care of me.
PSALM 27:10

Q&A

I am sexually active, and I have tried to stop, but it seems too hard. How can I stop?

You may think there is no hope to stop, and it may be difficult to stop, but you can. Most people who are sexually active outside of marriage are trying to meet a healthy need in an unhealthy way. Today's world tells you that sex is the answer for longings of love, affection, purpose, or acceptance. You've probably realized that sex has not met these needs in your life but has left you with a powerful desire to act out sexually.

Be honest with yourself and with God about your own needs, and ask God to fill your heart's empty spots. Invite God to heal any rejection, abuse, or abandonment in your life. Know that Jesus's cleansing blood makes you white as snow and that He can spiritually restore your virginity.

You may need to seek godly counsel with a pastor or counselor. You will also need to renew your mind by studying God's Word. Protect yourself from anything sexual in what you see, hear, and talk about. Continually exposing yourself to sexual influences is like trying to rid your body of poison while you're still drinking poison. Choose God's best today—He has the healing and the answers you need.

You have died, and your life is hidden with Christ in God. Christ is your life. . . . Therefore, put to death whatever is worldly in you: your sexual sin, perversion, passion, lust, and greed.
COLOSSIANS 3:3–5

Q&A

How can you help someone when she thinks she's fat but really she's skinny?

This person cannot see her true image in a mirror. Her perception of what she is seeing is confused. Your words of encouragement or confrontation will not change what she sees when she looks at herself. You will need to get this individual to talk about what she is going through emotionally. Perhaps you can help her explore why she is critical of her body.

If you can at least get this person to see that there are other things going on inside besides just her perception of how she looks, she may be able to see she needs help. Talking about surface issues will not help her change. Your friend has to take a deeper look (beyond the surface or what she sees with her eyes) to see that the image issue is not the real root of her struggle.

*Behold, You desire truth in the innermost being,
and in the hidden part You will make me know wisdom.*
PSALM 51:6 NASB

Q&A

If God loves me, then why did He let someone hurt me in a bad way when I was little? I need an answer before moving on.

Just like God works through people who are surrendered to Him, the devil works through people who are surrendered to him. The devil seeks to kill, steal, and destroy. In the person who hurt you, the devil found someone who was hurt and vulnerable enough to be used as a tool of pain and destruction in your life.

The devil wants to deceive you through your pain to believe that God does not love or care about you. Satan knows that hurts can keep you stuck in discouragement and disappointment with life and angry with God. But, God does love you, and His heart was broken by what happened to you. This book is just one of God's messages to you of His love and His desire to heal your pain.

Please understand that what happened to you did not come from the heart or mind of God. God desires to restore you to wholeness and shower you with a life of purpose so you are free to fulfill your destiny with confidence, peace, and joy. If you will let God, He will heal all your pain and change your life forever. Give Him an opportunity today.